Ron Mueck
Encounter

Ron Mueck
Encounter

The Art Gallery of New South Wales
acknowledges the Gadigal, the traditional
custodians of the Country on which it stands.

Since 1871, the Art Gallery of New South Wales has championed living Australian artists while reflecting and exploring perspectives from our place in the world. It is our honour to be staging *Ron Mueck: Encounter*, presenting the work of a living Australian – if truly international – artist, more than twenty years since his last solo exhibition in Sydney.

Encounter is an exhibition close to my heart. We began talking about developing a significant project with Ron Mueck in 2017, finally enticing him more than three years ago to once again present work on home soil. I was fortunate to visit him in his studio on the Isle of Wight. A visit entails a long day trip from London by train, ferry and taxi, but the pay-off is immersion in a wonderland of sculptural body parts, strangely familiar faces, precision tools and cardboard maquettes.

Among it all were multiple manifestations of the dogs that have been brewing as a subject for Mueck for several years. These first became public as the powerful three-dog sculpture *En Garde* in 2023, but Mueck had a more active and anxious scene in mind; Sydney became his opportunity to unleash his pack of eight fierce creatures for the first time as *Havoc*.

Havoc cements Mueck's shift in focus away from surface realism towards essential form and distilled action – the encounter – allowing more dynamic poses and complex groupings to result. With its palpable, snarling tension, this astonishing group feels markedly topical in our troubled and uncertain times.

Havoc joins a thoughtfully selected group of Mueck's stunningly realistic and intimate sculptures in one of the largest exhibitions of his career. With his skills honed through years as a puppet-maker, model-maker, animator and special effects master, Mueck completely redefined contemporary sculpture when he began exhibiting in the late 1990s. Together, the works in *Encounter* provide not only an important overview of Mueck's artistic development since those days, but trace the evolution of his new muscular distillations, situating works like *Havoc* within his long-term focus on empathy and affect.

Ron Mueck: Encounter is a reminder that an artist's care-filled reflection on our human condition within the wider world matters deeply. It also demonstrates the importance of art and galleries as places of fascination and emotional encounter.

I warmly congratulate Ron Mueck on his life-affirming exhibition. I extend my thanks to his exhibitions director, Charlie Clarke, who has worked insightfully and tirelessly with the Art Gallery team led by Jackie Dunn, senior curator of exhibitions, and Fatima Hijazi, exhibition manager. I also acknowledge Mueck's representative, Polly Robinson Gaer, executive director of Thaddaeus Ropac, London, for her close and continued involvement, and his friend and collaborator, the photographer and filmmaker Gautier Deblonde.

Instrumental in bringing this exhibition to life has been the invaluable support of the NSW Government through its tourism and events agency Destination NSW. I also acknowledge the many people, both within and beyond the Art Gallery, whose support made this exhibition and publication possible, and who share a belief in the boundless possibilities of art to foster deeper understanding and connection.

Maud Page
Director
Art Gallery of New South Wales

Enchanted encounters
Jackie Dunn

Preamble

For most of us, there is only the unattended
Moment, the moment in and out of time,
The distraction fit, lost in a shaft of sunlight

– TS Eliot, 1941[1]

Since first revitalising figurative sculpture in the late 1990s
with his meticulously crafted realism, Ron Mueck has
developed a sculptural language built on close observation
and emotional force. The Australian-born artist, who
began crafting puppets with his toy-making family before
establishing a career in film and television, has spent decades
creating lifelike figures and sculptures through a process of
drawing, modelling and painting. These creations, reflecting
inner worlds of private feeling with a disquieting power,
seem born not merely of skilful artistic process but of
magic. Scaled from the minute to the monumental, Mueck's
sculptures both record and create encounters – within
and between each work, with and between viewers – that
uncannily mirror our interpersonal human encounters, so
much so that we perceive them as interactions with the real.
      Coming more than twenty years after his last major
solo exhibition in Sydney, *Ron Mueck: Encounter* at the
Art Gallery of New South Wales presents new conceptual
and material developments in Mueck's practice as a
series of psychologically intense encounters that are also
viscerally physical, affective and empathic. With a focus on
relationship and intersubjectivity, *Encounter* reflects on the
humanist sensitivity and significance of his work within the
contemporary moment. In an age often characterised by
digital mediation, Mueck's sculptures return us to the bodily,
immediate and present moment of shared physical space.
And, in troubled times, his work's attentiveness to affect
and feeling, to the relationships between subjects, can be
recognised as expressing an ethics of empathy that sustains
his truly generative and enchanting encounters.

Sculpture / Encounter

Sculpture is not just an image of, but an entrance to, things … Sculpture is about the primal foundations of our sensory experience.

– F David Martin, 1976 [2]

To say that one merely looks at a Ron Mueck sculpture misses the mark. One *encounters* it. This is not just a matter of semantics but of experience; a phenomenological distinction rooted in the particular quality of presence these works command.

In 1998, shortly after his emergence as a visual artist, Mueck offered a remark, oft-quoted, that sums up the aspiration he nurtures for his art: 'Although I spend a lot of time on the surface, it's the life inside that I want to capture.' Less often quoted, but equally telling, is another comment from the same interview: 'I wanted to make something that a photograph wouldn't do justice to.'[3] Just what is it that a photograph wouldn't – couldn't – do justice to?

The answer is, at least in part, dimensionality. A photograph captures only one aspect of a moment, what something looks like, but not what it *feels* like to share its physicality – to walk around it and see it unfold in time and space. Curiously, in a photograph, Mueck's startling realism can trick the eye so that his figures look like sentient and corporeal human subjects – real people, but flattened, *imaged*. Meeting his figures in the flesh is something quite different. They have – they *are* – presences that demand acknowledgement. They are beings. Uncannily invested with an inner life, with stories folded into their skin, they occupy space as something (or someone) to be with, drawing our eyes and bodies into a tangible physical relationship, an embodied, fully dimensional exchange between object and viewer.

And yet Mueck is not a magician, even if his effects are magical. It is his skill as a *sculptor* that determines how perfectly or imperfectly he realises – makes real – his vision. His work is marked by the highest technical proficiency, is grounded in material knowledge and is steeped in a systematic conception of his artform. Mueck contends with both the long tradition of making figurative sculpture *and* with sculpture's philosophical demands that tease out the 'thingness' of matter, the weight of representation, the passage of time, the space of the body, the participation of the viewer.

Mueck's magic, if you like, is conjured from all sculpture's traits: tactility (felt and experienced through the skin), haptics (inviting us to explore more complex sensations perceptually) and proprioception (inviting an awareness of our body's position and movement in space). Mueck knows sculpture is primarily something that inhabits the same space as us as viewers, in dynamic relationship as we move through space, place and time. We may look first to his exceptionally wrought skin, his (in fact, painted) surfaces, but above all his work draws on sculpture's haptic potential – its call to *touch* – as something signally productive in suggesting a palpably *living* body. Standing before one of his material creations may provoke an almost primal urge to reach out, to verify the illusion, to find warmth or breath – and, in doing so, to be touched in return.[4]

So, Mueck calls attention to sculpture's oldest and most persistent ambition: the creation of presence. His lifelike figures don't just mimic the human form, they invite human encounter. They seem to return our look, to meet us in a suspended moment of recognition and intersubjective encounter that involves an exchange, an understanding that issues from an interaction with other bodies, whether human or material. And because they live inside social spaces – museums, galleries – our encounters with them are shared. In this way, they are more than representations, more than presences; they are an *event*.

Time / Event

Kairos was represented in a statue of bronze,
in which art vied with nature … We stood
speechless at the sight … and though it was void
of living sensation, it inspired the belief that it
had sensation dwelling within it …

– Callistratus, 3rd century CE [5]

In ancient Greece, Kairos was a minor god who personified
one of two concepts of time: the opportune or critical
moment. Unlike *chronos*, the steady, relentless tick of time's
absolute march, *kairos* refers to a fleeting moment, a sliver
of possibility, which has its roots in archery (as the point
through which an arrow must pass to hit its mark) and in
weaving (the moment yarn must be drawn through a soon-
to-close opening in the warp).[6] *Kairos* is that qualitative
character of time seized, timeliness, the charged instant
that comes only once, and never again.

Mueck's figures seem to dwell in this realm sharing
just such a sense of time. They are not archetypes or timeless
abstractions, but beings caught mid breath, mid thought,
mid life. Suspended at the peak of meaning, their sense of
stilled time gives them an affective force that echoes Homer's
conception of *kairos* in *The Iliad* as the vital place in the
body vulnerable to being hit to lethal effect. (Everything
we come to understand about *Young Couple* 2013, [pp 66–71],
for example, hinges on an encounter with an ambiguous
grasping gesture that stops time, a brief and fragile moment
that both condenses and stretches meaning.)

Callistratus's ancient reflection on the statue of
Kairos connects lifelikeness and liveliness, coupling mimetic
realism and artistic decision-making (catching the telling
moment). The awe he expressed at the 'sensation dwelling
within' the bronze, rendering him speechless, could easily
describe a contemporary viewer's encounter with a work by
Mueck. At the crux of Callistratus's account is the centuries-
old aspiration of figurative sculpture in the European
tradition and Mueck's singular achievement: to staunch
the flux of motion and catch the 'pregnant moment'. As
Gotthold Ephraim Lessing put it in his foundational work
on aesthetics, art should aim to depict the suggestive pause
caught between two instants, pregnant with the past and
yet to deliver the future; the moment of rising action.[7]

This is sculpture as the art of timing. Time, material
and emotion converge, so that beyond their breathtaking
detail and mimetic intensity, we might consider these
sculptures as temporal, bodily and affective events –
orchestrations, moments seized. Like Callistratus before
the statue of Kairos, we stand before Mueck's figures and
feel time thicken. We meet ghosts, stumble into bedrooms,
enter a dark place, feel the last heartbeat of a pig, get caught
in a dog fight. These scenes carry an understanding of
encounter as time and time as encounter: a coming-together,
a crossing of paths, a moment that might be confrontational,
tender or transformative; an opportune moment of intensity
that holds life for just a moment longer before it slips away.

Though sculpture is often thought of as the most
fixed of artforms, Mueck renders it strangely fluid. His work
reframes sculpture as a time-based art, not through actual
motion but through its ability to inhabit the significant interval
and arrest a moment that traverses past, present and future.
The stillness of his scenes is not inert but expectant, caught
in the narrow gap between what was and what is yet to
come. Urgent and intimate, those scenes ask to be witnessed
before the window closes, before the arrow hits, before the
moment is gone.

Hyperrealism / Realism

They aren't living persons, although it's nice to stand in front of them and be unsure whether they are or not ... I wouldn't be satisfied if they didn't have some kind of presence that made you think they're more than just objects.

– Ron Mueck, 2003 [8]

For decades, Mueck has been around the world and back as the poster child of 'hyperrealism' – a term that suggests not just reality, but reality enhanced, exaggerated to the point of *un*reality. Yet it is a label he resists.[9] Any unease with the term likely arises from its baggage: its association with glossy surface effects, with spectacle over substance, with the superficiality of its pop-ist origins. There's a sense, too, that hyperrealism carries the whiff of trickery – a clever sleight of hand rather than a deep emotional engagement.

Mueck's discomfort points to a dissatisfaction with the term's limitation regarding the intent of his practice. As his long-time studio collaborator Charlie Clarke observes, Mueck's fastidious commitment to detail – hair laid just so, freckles applied in perfectly random distribution – is not about showing off technical prowess. It's about preserving the illusion. A single inconsistency, however small, can break the spell.[10] Mueck's aim is not illusionism for its own sake, but *connection*: to bridge the gap between object and viewer, to hold attention long enough that something more profound might pass between them.

(It is true, of course, that Mueck leans into some of hyperrealism's strengths: the intensification of the aesthetic experience that paradoxically feels more real than real. He does this not least through his considerable skill as a painter, partly collapsing the traditional distinctions between sculpture and painting.)

If hyperrealism as a category – a term only coined in 1973[11] and most often linked to photorealist painters and, later, sculptors such as Duane Hanson (USA 1925–96) and John de Andrea (USA b1941) – feels too narrow for Mueck's purposes, the longer lineage of *realism* may offer a more fitting frame. Realism, in its many guises – whether the sensuous flesh of classical ancient Greek marbles, the entreaty to religious fervour guiding seventeenth-century Spanish polychromed sculptures, or the socially conscious naturalism of French nineteenth-century capital-R Realism – has always involved more than mere replication. As art historian Linda Nochlin reminds us:

Realism implies a system of values involving close investigation of particulars, a taste for ordinary experience in a specific time, place and social context ... Realism is more than and different from wilful virtuosity or the passive reflexivity of the mirror image ...[12]

For all its persuasive power, realism is inherently contradictory: an art based on truthfulness, objectivity and an unidealised confrontation with the world that has always been in a complicated relationship to 'the real'. Realism's very illusionism hinges at the exact point at which art and reality converge, swinging us between being taken in and becoming aware of the artifice. Mueck's alchemical concoctions of silicone, fibreglass and paint entice us to forget their fabrication, only to reassert it through scale, materiality or placement, reaffirming their condition as sculpture.[13]

And this, perhaps, is where Mueck's contribution feels most vital. In an age where reality itself is stretched out of shape and unrecognisable, he reminds us that realism has never been a simple mirror, more an artfully polished lens. As Mueck himself puts it, 'Sometimes, what feels right is not what actually is right.' He doesn't craft his realism to dully reproduce the human (and more recently, animal) body – that would just be duplication, he notes[14] – but engages in a deliberate act of selection, producing details and working at a chosen scale to build a believable entity. Mueck's realism, like all realisms, is a *choice*.[15]

The force of realist art has always been its way of pointing through and beyond appearances. Even now, as Mueck moves away from the exacting true-to-life surfaces of earlier works, the core of his realism as a kind of truth-seeking, not truth-copying, remains intact. He continues to touch the quick with a distinct form of encounter that moves through the tensions and contradictions within illusionism itself to allow for ambiguity.[16] Ultimately, Mueck's is a *version* of the real that makes visible aspects of experience that normal perception might miss, to serve what art historian Michael Fried calls 'the ultimate stakes of serious art – to attach us to reality'.[17]

Size / Scale

Size determines an object, but scale
determines art … Scale depends on one's
capacity to be conscious of the actualities
of perception.

– Robert Smithson, 1972 [18]

Mueck has little interest in working at life-size. 'We meet life-size people every day,' he once remarked – a casual dismissal that speaks volumes.[19] His figures, whether shrunken to an intimate, private degree or enlarged to a confronting immensity, explore the psychological implications of scale. They may appear startlingly lifelike, but they stop us, confounded, in our tracks: *Too small. Too large. Impossible.*

Scale, after all, is not some fixed attribute of an object but a matter of perception: relational, subjective – an experience filtered through the body and shaped by context. Perception of scale has often been understood as merely physical, our body its constant measure. Art historian TJ Clark deepens this understanding by noting that scale is a property of resemblance and comparison: 'Size is experienced as immediate, as given in the nature of things … Scale, on the other hand, is unabashedly metaphorical, and accepts size as a mere effect of representation.'[20] In Mueck's hands, scale is just such a figure of speech, one he deploys to move us into psychological space.

Figurative sculpture is a mode that connects scale and naturalism with uncanny results; keyed to our human bodies, it feels *always already* out of scale.[21] Playing with scale is not new to it, a point made by the late art historian Robert Rosenblum when writing on Mueck, citing Michelangelo's colossal *David* and Clodion's perfectly miniaturised tabletop sculptures as examples.[22] Yet, as Rachel Wells notes in her study of scale in contemporary sculpture, such historical examples were typically tethered to context – scaled to fit a piazza or an interior table.[23] Wells suggests Mueck's work, by contrast, emerges from a postmodern condition in which scale itself is destabilised. She identifies in this contemporary sculptural tendency a crisis of certainty: a resistance to fixed values, a challenge to the stable interpretation of the real.[24]

Wells turns to Susan Stewart, the literary theorist who has done much to map the symbolic terrain of scale. Stewart connects 'the miniature to the ideal and the gigantic to the grotesque', defining 'the miniature as contained, the gigantic as container.'[25] The miniature she aligns with intimacy, domesticity, interiority, what is 'overly cultural'. The gigantic, meanwhile, stretches outward, towards 'infinity, exteriority, the public, and the overly natural'.[26] Consider Mueck's intimate *Spooning Couple* (pp 42–47) with its quiet, bed-bound tenderness, with Stewart's notes in mind: 'The miniature offers us a transcendent vision which is known only through the visual … we can only stand outside, looking in, experiencing a type of tragic distance.'[27] Or his *Big Man* (pp 30–33), that easily dwarfs us: 'the gigantic transforms the [viewer's] body into miniature … we are enveloped by the gigantic, surrounded by it, enclosed within its shadow.'[28]

Mueck's use of scale is not directly allegorical, nor is it programmatic or strictly symbolic. Rather, the scale he lands on for a piece is part of a creative process that unfolds intuitively in the studio, and always in service to his deeper aim: to disturb habitual seeing. As he explains, mimetic realism alone doesn't carry emotional weight, 'the emotional impact comes from how the figure occupies space and interacts with the viewer'.[29] His scale alterations, therefore, are made to simply settle the work's own 'correct' size and, at the same time, act as profound and disconcerting disruptions.

Mueck's figures – impossibly real in appearance thus impossibly wrong in size – draw us in with the believability of the illusion, then throw us with the incongruity of the scale. The result is a perceptual dissonance that compels us to resolve the contradiction. As theorist Anne Cranny-Francis writes, this tension stimulates us into self-reflexivity, making us hyperaware of both our own 'embodied being and of the fundamentally embodied and interconnected nature of being'.[30] In confronting these not-quite-right bodies, we grow more attuned to our own.

Affect / Empathy

The body is our general medium for
having a world.

– Maurice Merleau-Ponty, 1962 [31]

Social and literary theorist Roland Barthes once named
that haunting element in a photograph which touches us
most deeply the 'punctum' – a point of impact that 'rises
from the scene, shoots out of it like an arrow, and pierces'.[32]
Mueck's sculptures seem similarly armed. Not content to
merely resemble life, they send out their own arrows – small,
piercing details that gently wound. How, we might ask,
do these sculptures achieve such a charge? How do they
become the complex matrices of affect and empathy that
elicit a gasp, a squirm, the pain of recognition or a held
breath, to function as living presences among us? What
would it mean to take them seriously, not only as aesthetic
objects but as participants in a genuinely intersubjective
exchange?

That might sound unhinged. After all, these figures
are not alive. They are silicone, fibreglass, pigment and
artificial hair – exquisite fictions. And yet, the power they
hold over us cannot be explained away as our being either
deluded or fabulist. Mueck's realism tugs at something
both deeper and stranger than trickery and to consider
it, we might summon the term 'affect'. Most readily
understood as a feeling, affect is a somatic response or
pre-cognitive form of embodied knowing – a gut reaction,
a visceral intensity, something 'synonymous with *force* or
forces of encounter', even when those forces are subtle,
barely perceptible: 'ordinary and its extra-'.[33]

Literary theorist Charles Altieri helps us bridge
affect and aesthetics. He proposes that affect includes
an 'accompanying imaginative dimension', one that
accounts for the complex heightened and intense affective
states produced by works of art. Arguing we are often
too eager to interpret, he cites a 'tendency to overread
for "meaning" while underreading the specific modes of
affective engagement presented by works of art'.[34] Rather,
we might look to the piercing force of affects and ask
what art *does* to us.

Mueck declines to interpret his work, offering no
didactic certainties and leaving his sculptures open –
radically so – to the full spectrum of the viewer's personal
associations. The works don't offer themselves up for
decoding either, rather they overwhelm, disturb, delight.
Their power lies precisely in this excess – or, as Altieri
puts it, in their *rapture*. They are not reducible to symbolic
interpretation, knowable, *readable*; they are concentrated
moments of affective intensity only able to be *felt*.

Theorist Sara Ahmed argues that affects and emotions
are cultural and social, as well as individual; they are 'sticky',
accumulating emotional weight, values and meanings which
adhere and circulate.[35] Emotions are not only private things,
but work 'between bodies', across skin, gesture, atmosphere,
time, communities. Mueck's sculptures are sticky objects. His
remarkable figures, cultivated in the studio to become rich
in affect, function as particularly potent sites of emotional
density that invite attachment to our own sensations and
stories, layering them with the sediment of experience.
Mueck's refusal to offer interpretations only intensifies this
layering. With no script to follow, each viewer brings their
own psychic weather and embodied histories: a hard-won
pregnancy, a lost parent, an adolescent brush with shame.
The sculptures don't (only) *represent* these experiences, they
absorb them and are charged in the exchange, becoming
both repositories and signs of collective feeling. And all of
this takes place in public, so that as we move with other
bodies – both sculpted and human – in the gallery space, its
social dynamics are transformed.

When viewers report believing they might wake the
sleeping *Man in Blankets* (pp 26–29) or send the skittish teenage
Ghost (pp 18–21) scuttling if they meet her eye, they are not
whimsical imaginings. They are signs of what has been called
a 'living presence response', whereby:

> Viewers react to works of art as if they are living and
> acting persons not because they have come alive for
> some miraculous or supernatural reason, or because
> these spectators suffer from cognitive or semiotic
> confusion … but because they *experience* the work
> of art as living [36]

(and react this way *even when* they know the work is not
living). This experience has deep roots. Across centuries,
people have spoken to statues, kissed them, wept before
them, claimed they breathed, bled, listened. Mueck's
sculptures sit squarely within this lineage. They blur the
boundaries between person and object, presence and
representation, animate and inanimate. They provoke us into
a form of enchantment that is not irrational, but relational.

Living presence response is an extension of the
'contagious' dual quality of being *moved by* and *moving
towards* that is shared across all our inter-human encounters
and that we understand as empathy. Empathy, as it turns
out, has aesthetic origins. The term was first used in the
nineteenth century to describe how viewers *feel into* works
of art – how we animate objects through a kind of empathic
projection. As philosopher Robert Vischer wrote in 1873,
'I can think my way into [an object], mediate its size with my
own, stretch and expand, bend and confine myself to it.' [37]

In Mueck's work, this tradition of objects coming
alive through empathic projection finds new expression, but
not as uncritical sentimentality. What he invites is closer
to what art theorist Jill Bennett calls 'empathic vision' – a
critical spectatorship that implicates the self in the act of
seeing. Being touched in this way by a sculpture is a 'process
of "seeing feeling" where feeling is both imagined and
regenerated through an encounter with the artwork',
to create an ethical space of engagement.[38]

Evolution / Life

[E]cological art … must include ugliness
and disgust, and haunting weirdness,
and a sense of unreality as much as of reality.

– Timothy Morton, 2018 [39]

Recently, Mueck's focus has shifted. Where once he pursued an almost obsessive virtuosity in rendering the body's exterior surfaces – every wrinkle, hair and fingernail – he now seeks to conjure the 'life inside' almost exclusively through its 'body language': those movements and postures by which attitudes and feelings are communicated. The subject, Mueck seems to suggest to us, lives not (only) in the surface, but in form itself; not in details, but in the gestalt of their sum immediately perceived as a whole. This signals a subtle yet profound evolution in Mueck's sculptural thinking. He is distilling his enduring concerns into a new and precise choreography of gesture, posture and pose as carriers of emotional and psychological content, and as markers of an event. (Of course, this may always have been the case – that the 'sculpture' of Mueck's figures spoke first to us with visceral impact, only later to be deepened and sustained by the hyperreal 'painting' of their surfaces.)

At the (dark) heart of the exhibition is *Havoc* (pp 86–91): two packs of dogs locked in frenzied combat on the brink of mutual destruction. These fighting dogs are skin-pricklingly visceral, dramatically baroque and menacing (no, *more than* menacing – this is no mere threat of a fight, but the main event). In their snarling, weighty, mythic forms, we glimpse traces of naturalistic surface treatment in a flash of colour in tooth and maw, just enough to animate and electrify. Yet in the main, these grouped figures inhabit the monochrome realm of classical statuary, a neutral ground against which pose and body language emerge with striking clarity: gestures of hostile readiness (ears pinned back), postures of aggression (heads low, teeth bared), and hackles hand-carved to tremble with affect. The dogs project an almost palpable existential threat.

Deciding when a work is finished is no simple task for any artist. For Mueck, 'finished' used to mean when a figure could no longer be made more 'real'. *chicken/man* (pp 76–81) represents the apogee of this pore-level illusionism – an endpoint that preceded a conscious paring back. In *chicken/man*, viewers are drawn close by the fidelity of, say, facial stubble and compelled to scrutinise; in *Havoc*, the beasts' swallowing scale and warring poses arrest us with a primal immediacy. Mueck's reorientation may signal a reassessment of his love for hyperreal detailing, but his concern remains a probing test of what it means to evoke 'the real'. What might restraint yield, when form takes precedence over flawlessly realised skin? Can our attention still be held? And how much detail is necessary to stir our emotional response?

The dogs stand alongside another new work, *This Little Piggy* (pp 82–85) – a dynamic tableau that underscores the violence of contemporary human life at the heart of Mueck's current concerns – to increase the number of non-human subjects in Mueck's cast. Such cross-species encounters provoke reflection. As John Berger – whose collection of stories about brutal traditional life in rural France, *Pig Earth*, inspired *This Little Piggy* – writes, animals first entered the human imagination 'as messengers and promises'; he continues: 'If the first metaphor was animal, it was because the essential relation between man and animal was metaphoric.'[40] Berger notes that animals, both like and unlike us, carry a significant symbolic load on our behalf, a point picked up by writer Ceridwen Dovey:

> Berger's insight [was] that writers sometimes turn to *animal* narrators, or use animals as metaphors, at moments of emotional excess. When there is an overload of feeling, such that for a human things become unsayable, or 'indescribable' … We give voice to animals – and objects! – in order to be able to speak in symbolic terms about ourselves.[41]

Seen in this light, Mueck's recent 'animal turn' opens new registers of content and affect perhaps too difficult to assign to the human. Dogs, in particular, hold a unique symbolic cultural position as wild and domestic, threatening and protective. In folklore and fairytales, they are guardians of thresholds: between worlds, life and death, the known and the unknown. (The three-headed Cerberus, guardian of the underworld, reverberates in *Havoc*.) Dogs evoke this mythic dimension yet remain grounded in everyday reality – creatures both close to us (on our laps) and distantly other. *These* dogs are at once territorial street fighters and ghosts conjured from some ancient source, from memory itself.[42]

This new work signals more than an expansion of subject matter or a shift to restrained surfaces in Mueck's practice. It continues his recent expansion to the group form after years creating solitary figures or pairs (and this time, demands we join that group and step into the fray). Most appreciably, it expresses a veiled but potent commentary on our current social climate – a strong undercurrent often overlooked in Mueck's work. His constant aim has been a sincere exploration of the human condition, but to that he now brings a sense of urgency and a freer, if still enigmatic, critical voice. Encountering *Havoc* sparks a visceral anxiety that arises from evolutionary depths to resonate with our own eco-socio-political fears and generalised perception of precarity and global crisis. Are these dogs – risen from the past, here among us, and heralding a dangerous future – external threats, or manifestations of our own capacity for violence? As ever with Mueck, the work's disconcerting power lies precisely in its refusal to resolve this ambiguity. It forces us as viewers to confront our own position relative to both individual and collective aggression.

Everyday life is a life lived on the level of
surging affects, impacts suffered or barely
avoided. It takes everything we have. But it
also spawns a series of little somethings
dreamed up in the course of things.

– Kathleen Stewart, 2007 [43]

In this state, we don't just look or observe – we are
enchanted. And for Bennett, enchantment is not whimsy,
but a rigorous affective state: 'a moment of pure presence'
in which chronological time is briefly suspended, and we
find ourselves 'transfixed, spellbound'.[48] Mueck stills time
so we might pay attention and give ourselves over to the
enchanting power of the sculptural encounter – the charged
moments, felt between subjects, when art is a conduit for
the real. This is where Mueck's power resides: not in his
ability to reproduce reality, but in his ability to *reanimate* it –
to awaken our capacity to meet the world, and each other,
with feeling.

In *Ordinary affects*, anthropologist Kathleen Stewart called
for renewed attention to the emotional textures of daily
life. She seeks out the affective dimensions that vitalise
our lives and animate the ordinary; the small moments and
overlooked forces that shape how we feel our way through
the world. Ordinary affects are both 'public feelings that
begin and end in broad circulation' and 'the stuff that
seemingly intimate lives are made of' – volatile, vibrant,
messy, provisional things. [44] Affects, she writes, 'work not
through "meanings" per se, but rather ... pick up density
and texture as they move ... Their significance lies in the
intensities they build and in what thoughts and feelings they
make possible.'[45] One could say the same of Mueck's work.

Mueck's sculptures ask us to reverse our habitual
inattention. They pull us in close to register sagging flesh,
tensed knuckles, tiny blemishes and veins beneath the skin;
just familiar enough to draw us in, just strange enough
to hold us there. Leaning in, recoiling in recognition,
or gathering round in shared astonishment, we come
together in a gallery space now activated to become
emotionally charged, politically heedful and ethically
potent. Mueck's efforts to move beyond representation as
a barrier between us and the living world draw us into a
state of attentiveness, to find and experience encounters
that exceed the mere reproduction of reality. His is an
invitation to a different mode of attunement to the real:
to take seriously the extraordinary ordinary. Catching us
in moments of pause or transition, his art asks us to see
ourselves and others – human or material – as vulnerable,
weary, depressed, anxious, insecure, grieving, amused,
playful, curious ... It asks us to *notice*. And that act of
noticing opens a portal to our world experienced differently,
a world made strange and newly intimate.

This strange new world takes account of the power
of things – what philosopher Jane Bennett calls the 'vibrant
matter' of non-human entities and forces. Mueck's figures
sit at the threshold where 'human being and thinghood
overlap', as sites of entanglement.[46] Resonating with the
energetic vitality of material objects, sculptures become
participants. They hold what Bennett terms 'thing-power',
filled with their own animacy and the magnetic agency
of things that produce effects. When things and bodies
resonate through the meeting of their sheer physical
presences, our experience of what it is to be 'human' can
be 'altered, recomposed'.[47]

1 Excerpt from the TS Eliot poem, 'The dry salvages', *Four quartets*, Faber and Faber, London, 1970 (1944), p 44.

2 F David Martin, 'The autonomy of sculpture', *Journal of Aesthetics and Art Criticism*, vol 34, no 3, Wiley-Blackwell, New Jersey, 1976, pp 284–85.

3 Ron Mueck, quoted in Judith Palmer, 'Eyeball to eyeball with Mueck and his works', *The Independent*, 2 Jun 1998, p 3.

4 Cultural theorist Anne Cranny-Francis has written extensively on Mueck, touch and the slippage of Cartesian subjectivity that his work induces. See Cranny-Francis, 'Sculpture as deconstruction: the aesthetic practice of Ron Mueck', *Visual Communication*, vol 12, no 1, 2013, doi.org/10.1177/1470357212462672, accessed 22 Oct 2024.

5 Callistratus, 'On the statue of opportunity at Sicyon', *Ekphrases (Descriptions)*, trans Arthur Fairbanks, Harvard University Press, Cambridge, Mass, 1960 (1931), p 397. Callistratus's descriptions are thought to have been written in 3rd or 4th century CE.

6 Eric Charles White, cited in Emma Cocker, 'Kairos time: the performativity of timing and timeliness … or; between biding one's time and knowing when to act', paper presented at the first biennial PARSE conference, University of Gothenburg, Sweden, 6 November 2015, published by PARSE – Platform for Artistic Research Sweden, 2015, p 2, irep.ntu.ac.uk/id/eprint/27462/1/4697_Cocker.pdf, accessed 2 Jun 2025.

7 Gotthold Ephraim Lessing declared the plastic arts 'can use but a single moment of an action, and must therefore choose the most pregnant one, the one most suggestive of what has gone before and what is to follow'; Lessing, *Laocoon: an essay upon the limits of painting and poetry*, trans Ellen Frothingham, Little, Brown, and Company, Boston, 1910 (1766), p 92.

8 Mueck quoted in Sarah Tanguy, 'The progress of *Big Man*: a conversation with Ron Mueck', *Sculpture*, 1 Jul 2003, sculpturemagazine.art/the-progress-of-big-man-a-conversation-with-ron-mueck, accessed 4 May 2025.

9 Or more precisely, Mueck does not wish for his work to be glossed within the context of hyperrealism; conversation with author, 6 Nov 2024.

10 Conversation with author, 6 Nov 2024.

11 Belgian art dealer Isy Brachot is said to have coined the term *hyperréalisme* (hyperrealism) as the title of a 1973 exhibition at his gallery in Brussels. It featured, among others, several American photorealist painters.

12 Linda Nochlin, 'From the archives: the realist criminal and the abstract law', *Art in America*, 1 Sep 1973, artnews.com/art-in-america/features/the-realist-criminal-and-the-abstract-law-63236, accessed 1 Jun 2025.

13 See also Naomi Schor on American sculptor Duane Hanson: 'taken to its logical conclusion (and beyond), realism in sculpture can only self-deconstruct, give rise to a sort of metasculpture that comments on its own means of deception'; Schor, *Reading in detail: aesthetics and the feminine*, Routledge, London, 2007, p 173.

14 Tanguy 2003.

15 As Roland Barthes declared, 'the real is never anything but an inference; when we declare we are copying reality, this means that we choose a certain inference and not certain others: realism is, at its very inception, subject to the responsibility of a choice'; Barthes, 'Literature today: answers to a questionnaire in *Tel Quel*', *Critical essays*, trans Richard Howard, Northwestern University Press, Evanston, 1972, p 159.

16 See also Jennifer Friedlander for a paper on the 'potential for realism to contribute to a visual politics' (citing Mueck directly); Friedlander, 'Imperfecting the illusion: belief and the aesthetic destruction of reality', *Discourse*, vol 35, no 3, 2013, p 397, doi.org/10.13110/discourse.35.3.0384, accessed 1 Jun 2025.

17 Michael Fried, *Four honest outlaws: Sala, Ray, Marioni, Gordon*, Yale University Press, New Haven/London, 2011, p 24.

18 Robert Smithson, 'The spiral jetty' in Gyorgy Kepes (ed), *Arts of the environment*, George Braziller, New York, 1972, available holtsmithson foundation.org/spiral-jetty-1, accessed 1 Jul 2025.

19 Tanguy 2003.

20 TJ Clark, cited by Rachel Wells, *Scale in contemporary sculpture: enlargement, miniaturisation and the life-size*, Ashgate, Farnham, 2013, p 14; see also p 161.

21 We could extend this to all art, per anthropologist Claude Levi-Strauss, who considered it to be a miniaturisation (a 'scale model') of some aspect of the existing world; cited by Wells 2013, p 5.

22 Robert Rosenblum, 'Ron Mueck's bodies and souls', *Ron Mueck*, exh cat, Fondation Cartier pour l'art contemporain, Paris, 2005, p 68.

23 Wells 2013, p 2.

24 Wells 2013, pp 38–46.

25 Susan Stewart, *On longing: narratives of the miniature, the gigantic, the souvenir, the collection*, Duke University Press, Durham/London, 1993, p 71; also cited by Wells 2013, p 11.

26 Stewart 1993, p 70.

27 Stewart 1993, p 71.

28 Stewart 1993, p 71; see also p 68, for Mueck's insistence on plinths for his smaller works: 'As is the case with all models, it is absolutely necessary that Lilliput be an island. The miniature world remains perfect and uncontaminated by the grotesque so long as its absolute boundaries are maintained.'

29 Mueck, quoted in Jenny Raven, 'Ron Mueck: faces, bodies and flesh', Raven – Contemporary Home & Garden, 11 Dec 2024, ravencontemporary.com.au/artists/faces-bodies-flesh-contemporary-take-portraiture, accessed 24 Dec 2024 (webpage is no longer active).

30 Cranny-Francis 2013, p 12.

31 Maurice Merleau-Ponty, *Phenomenology of perception*, trans Colin Smith, Routledge & Kegan Paul, London, 1962 (1945), p 169.

32 Roland Barthes, *Camera lucida: reflections on photography*, trans Richard Howard, Hill and Wang, New York, 1981, p 26.

33 Gregory J Seigworth & Melissa Gregg, 'An inventory of shimmers' in Melissa Gregg & Gregory J Seigworth (eds), *The affect theory reader*, Duke University Press, Durham/London, 2010, pp 1–2.

34 Charles Altieri, *The particulars of rapture: an aesthetics of the affects*, Cornell University Press, Ithaca, 2003, p 2.

35 Sara Ahmed, 'Affective economies', *Social Text*, Duke University Press, Durham, vol 22, no 2, 2004, p 117.

36 Caroline van Eck, 'Living statues: Alfred Gell's *Art and agency*, living presence response and the sublime', *Art History*, Oxford University Press, vol 33, no 4, Sep 2010, p 646, doi.org/10.1111/j.1467-8365.2010.00756.x, accessed 1 Jun 2025.

37 Robert Vischer, 'On the optical sense of form: a contribution to aesthetics' in HF Mallgrave & Eleftherios Ikonomou (intro & trans), *Empathy, form, and space: problems in German aesthetics, 1873–1893*, The Getty Center for the History of Art and the Humanities, Santa Monica, 1994, pp 104–05.

38 It must be stated that Jill Bennett's focus is on visual art produced in the context of trauma: see Bennett, *Empathic vision: affect, trauma, and contemporary art*, Stanford University Press, Stanford, 2005, p 41.

39 Timothy Morton, *Being ecological*, Penguin Press, London, 2018, p 138.

40 John Berger, 'Why look at animals?' (1977), *About looking*, Pantheon Books, New York, 1980, pp 2–5.

41 Ceridwen Dovey, 'Telling stories from the perspectives of objects', *Sydney Review of Books*, 19 Feb 2023, sydneyreviewofbooks.com/essays/telling-stories-from-the-perspectives-of-objects, accessed 1 Jun 2025.

42 For such large forms, Mueck now sculpts first in the computer – a digital but otherwise 'traditional' form of modelling – producing routed forms he then brings to life by hand-carving and surface-finishing. The dogs in *Havoc* also carry a ghost of their digital origins in the slight sci-fi edge of their forms.

43 Kathleen Stewart, *Ordinary affects*, Duke University Press, Durham/London, 2007, p 9.

44 Stewart 2007, p 2.

45 Stewart 2007, p 3.

46 Jane Bennett, *Vibrant matter: a political ecology of things*, Duke University Press, Durham/London, 2010, p 4.

47 Jane Bennett, 'Encounters with an art-thing', *Evental Aesthetics 3*, no 3, 2015, p 105, salvageartinstitute.org/JaneBennett_EncountersWithanArtThing_eventalaesthetics_20150704.pdf, accessed 12 Jun 2025.

48 Jane Bennett, *The enchantment of modern life: attachments, crossings, and ethics*, Princeton University Press, Princeton/Oxford, 2001, p 5; the phrase 'moment of pure presence' is from American academic Philip Fisher. For Bennett, '… enchantment involves … a surprising encounter, a meeting with something that you did not expect and are not fully prepared to engage. Contained within this surprise state are (1) a pleasurable feeling of being charmed by the novel and as yet unprocessed encounter and (2) a more *unheimlich* (uncanny) feeling of being disrupted or torn out of one's default sensory-psychic-intellectual disposition. The overall effect of enchantment is a mood of fullness, plenitude, or liveliness, a sense of having had one's nerves or circulation or concentration powers tuned up or recharged …', Bennett 2001, p 5.

Plates

Ghost 1998/2014
202 × 65 × 99 cm

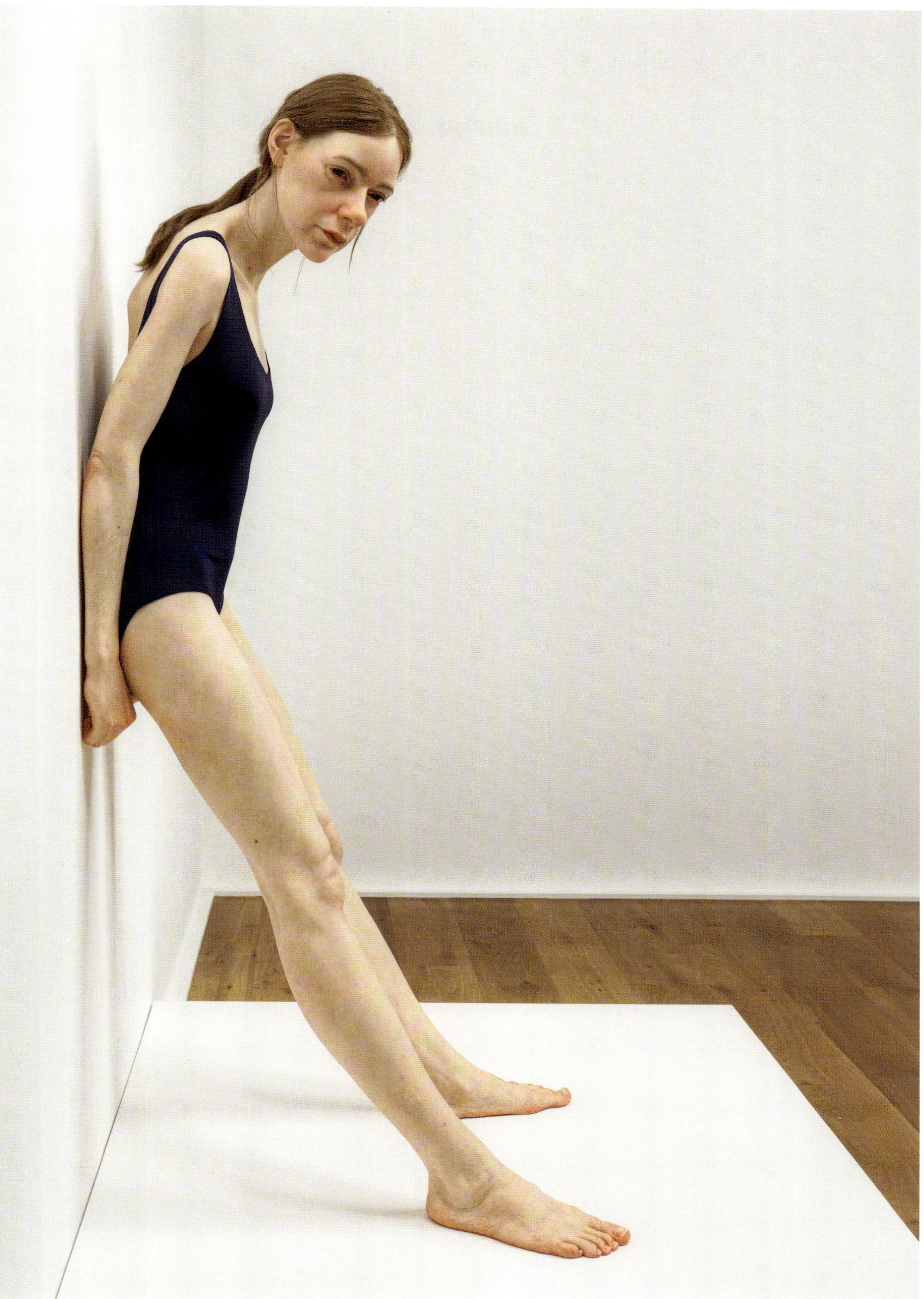

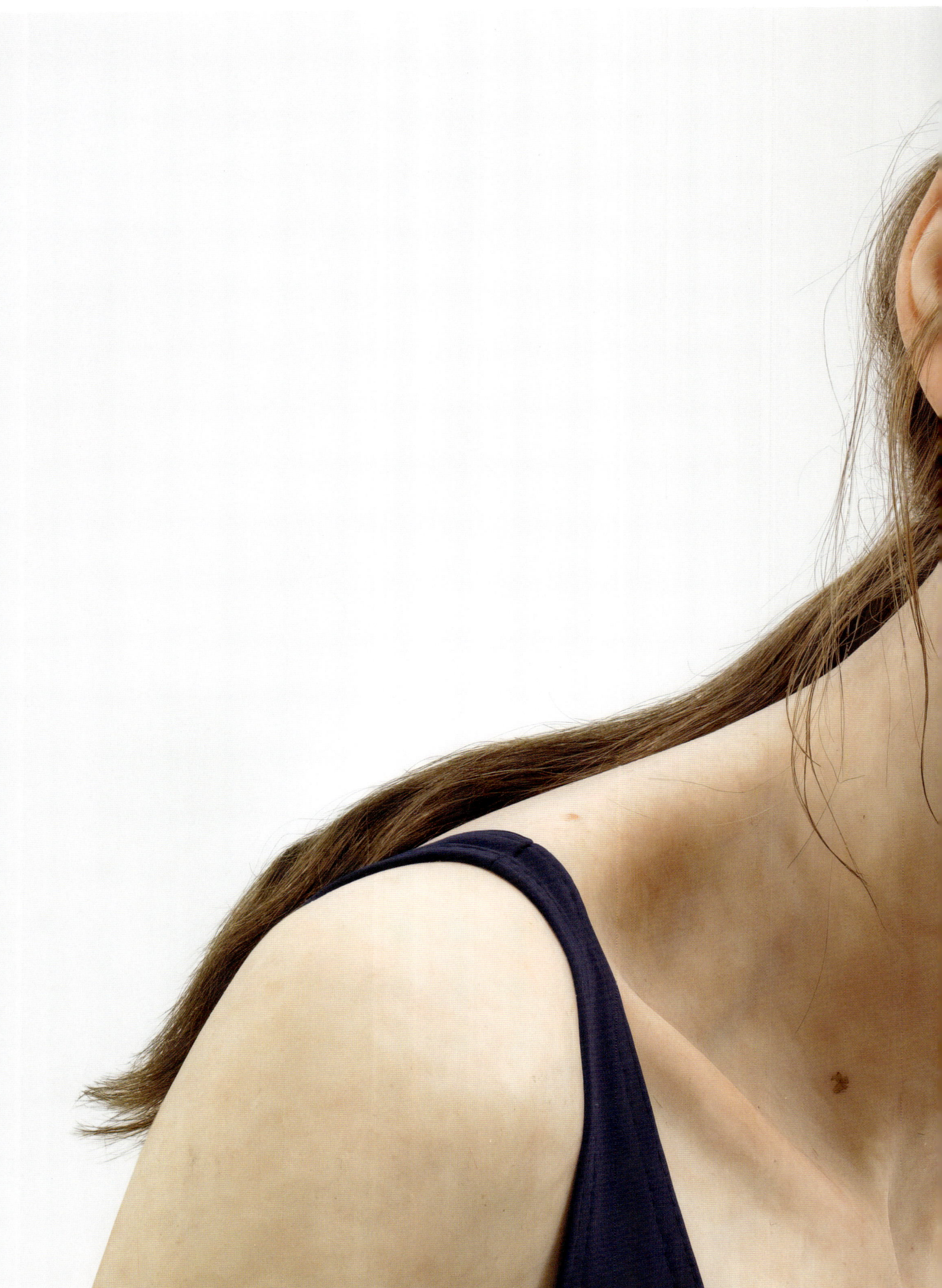

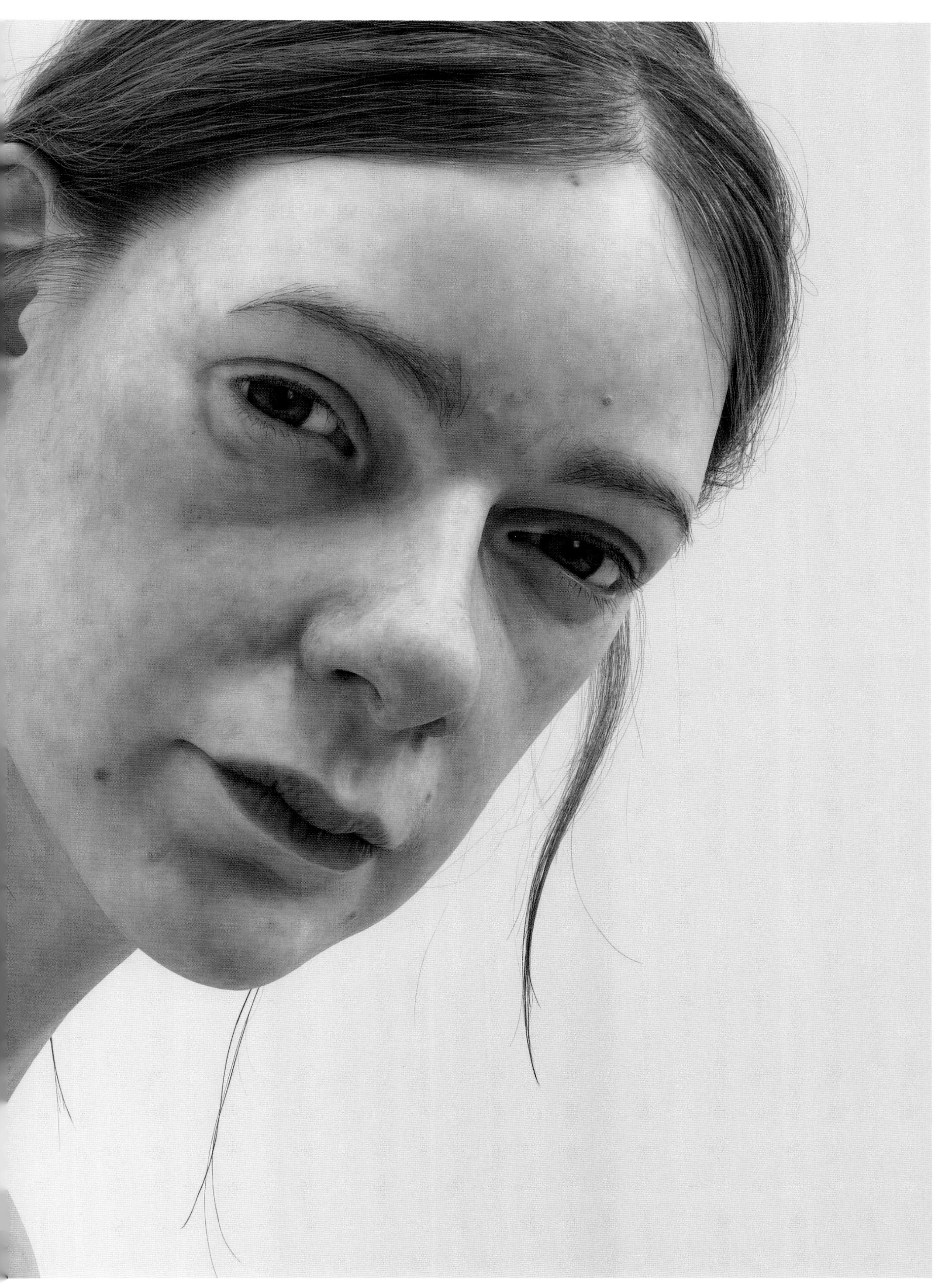

Crouching Boy in Mirror 1999–2002
43 × 46 × 28 cm figure; 46 × 56 cm mirror

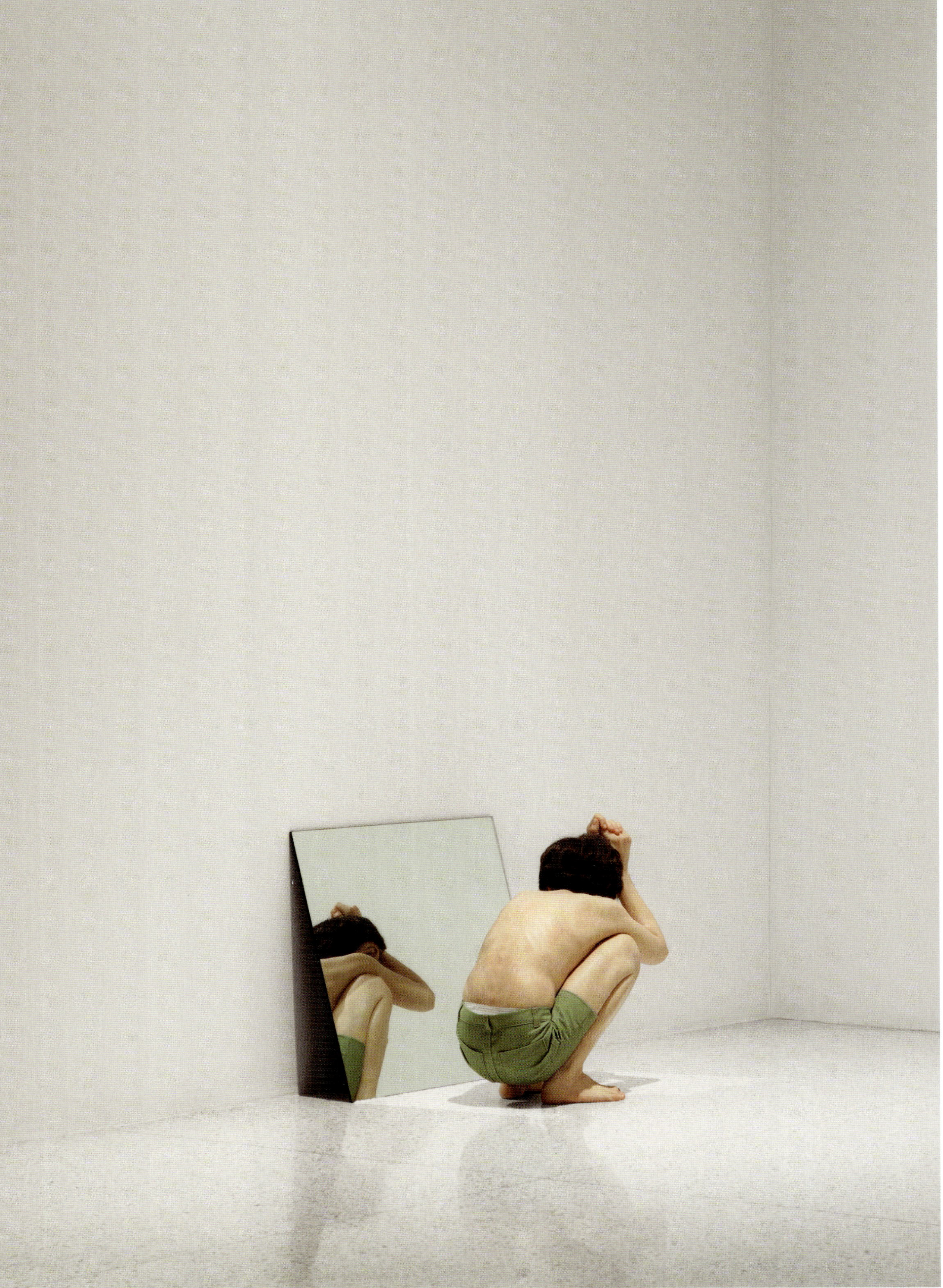

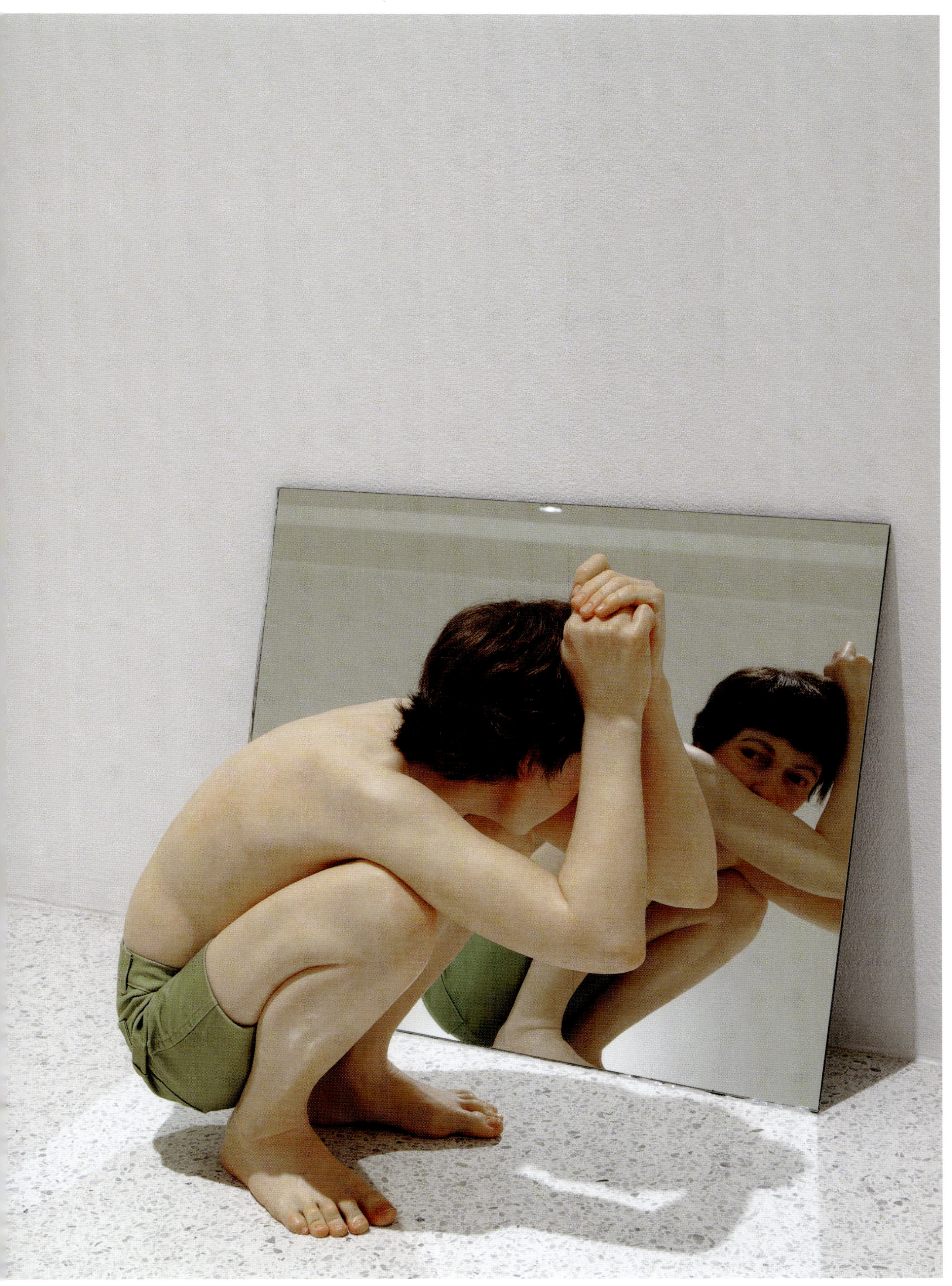

Man in Blankets 2000
38 × 46 × 71 cm

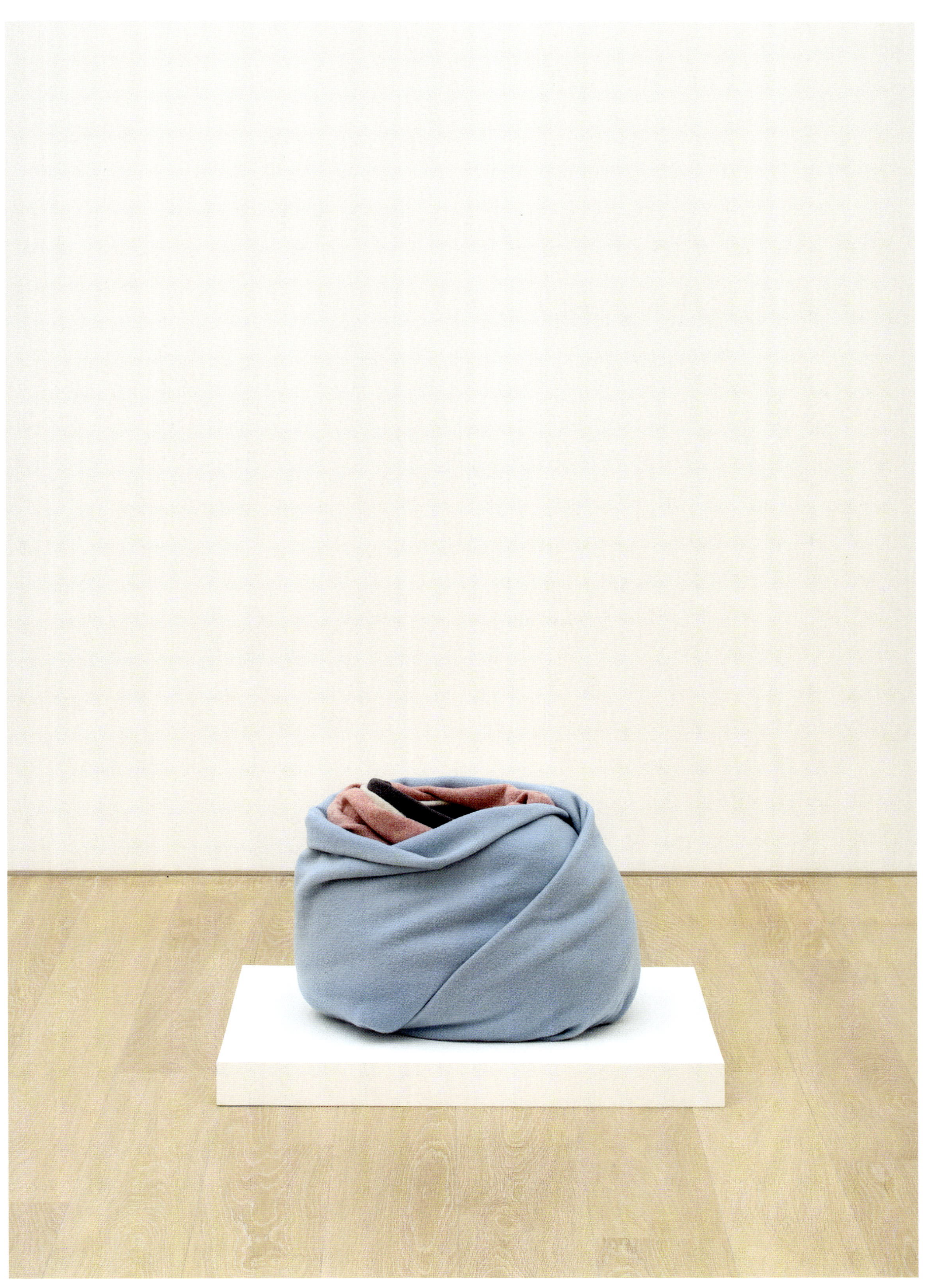

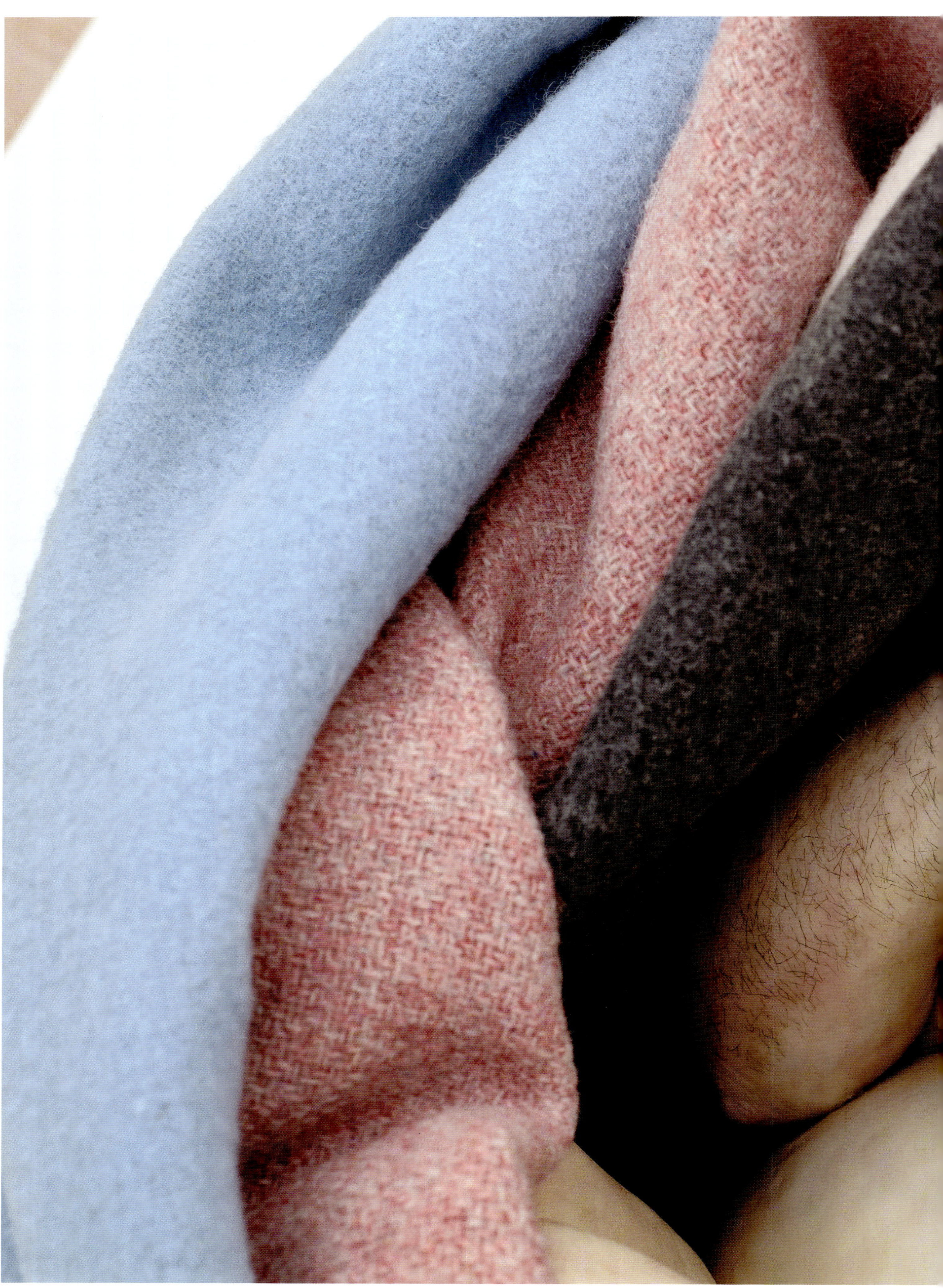

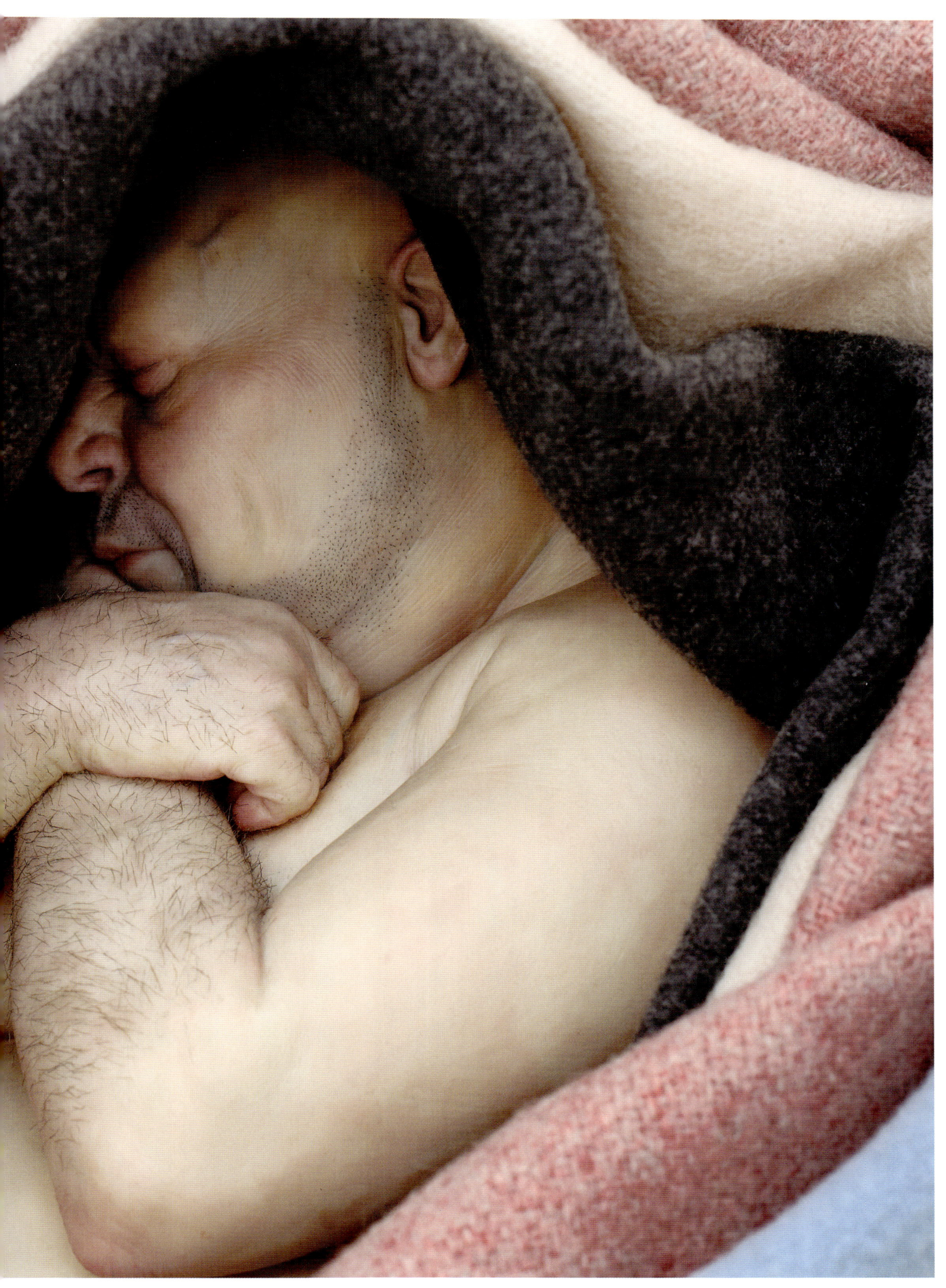

Big Man 2000
204 × 121 × 205 cm

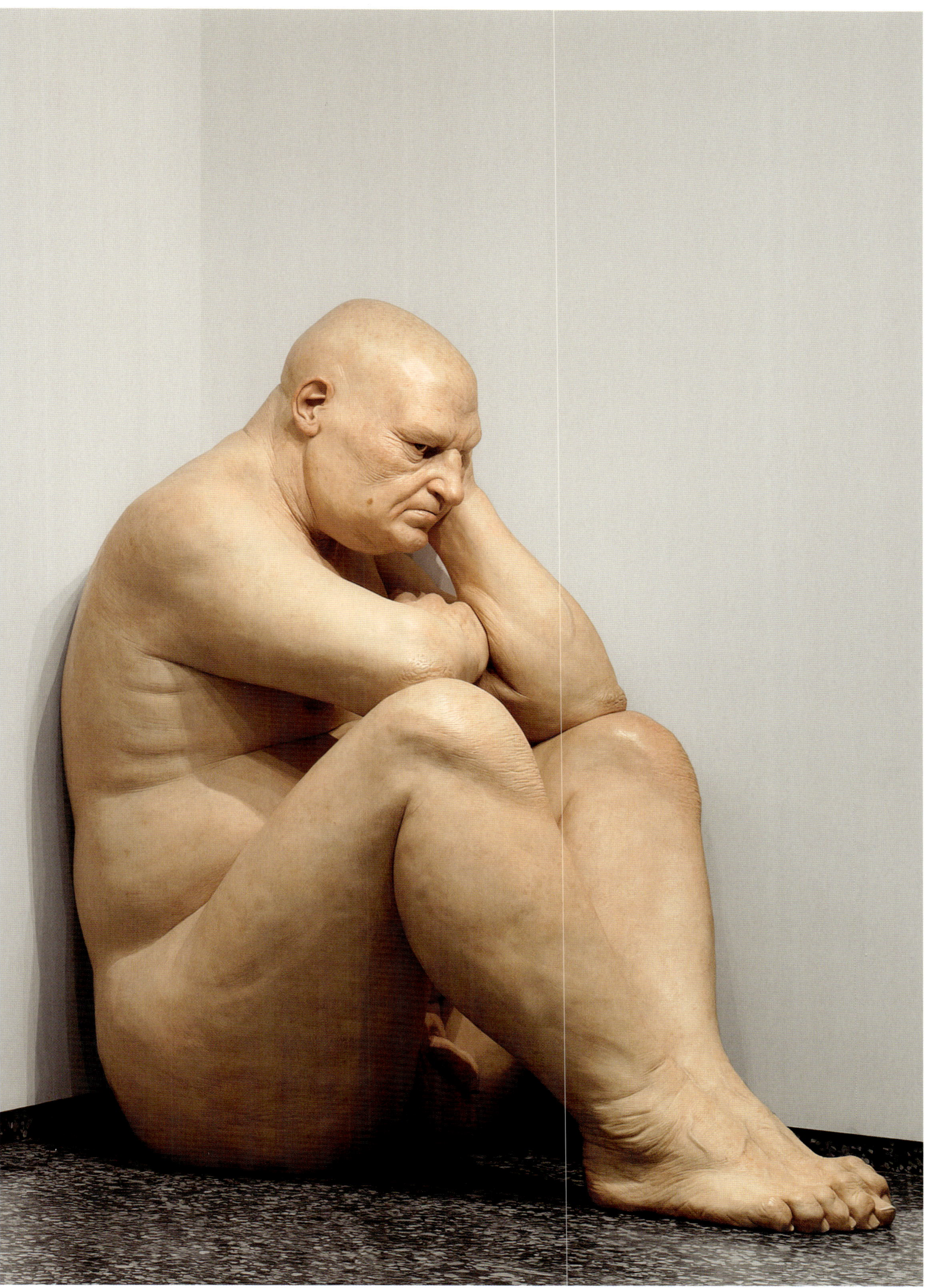

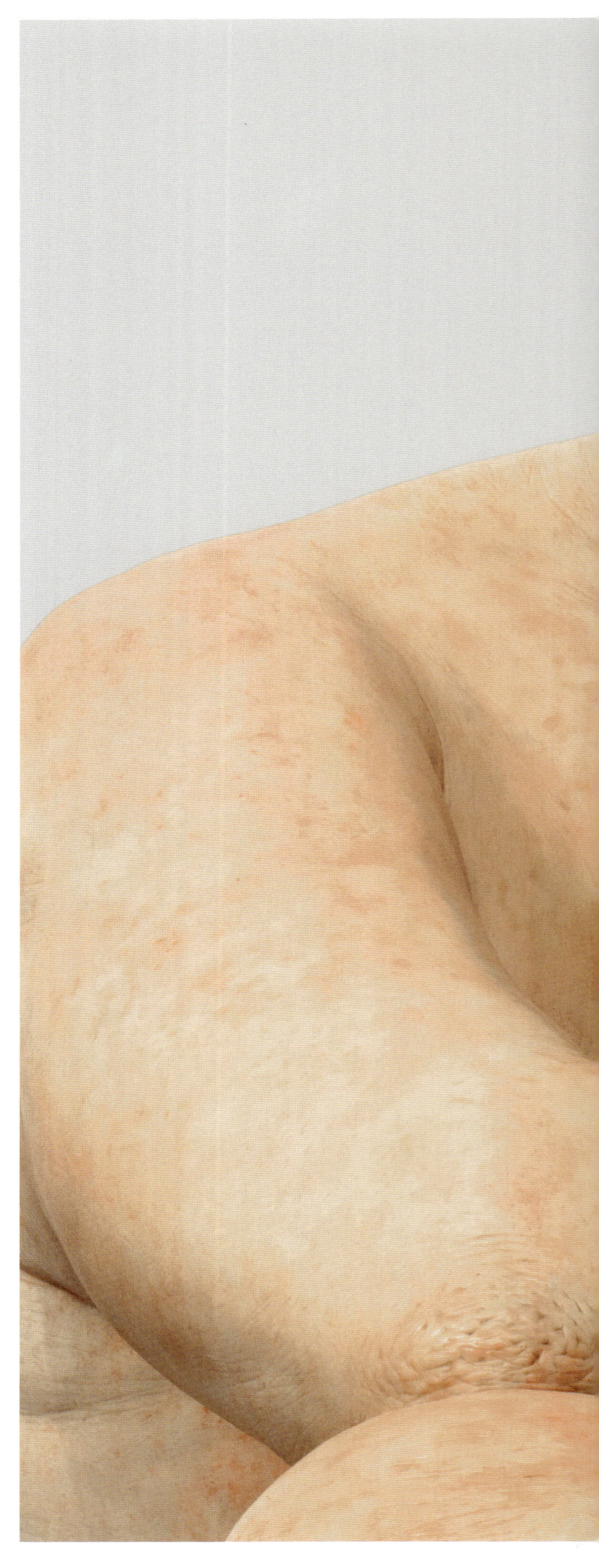

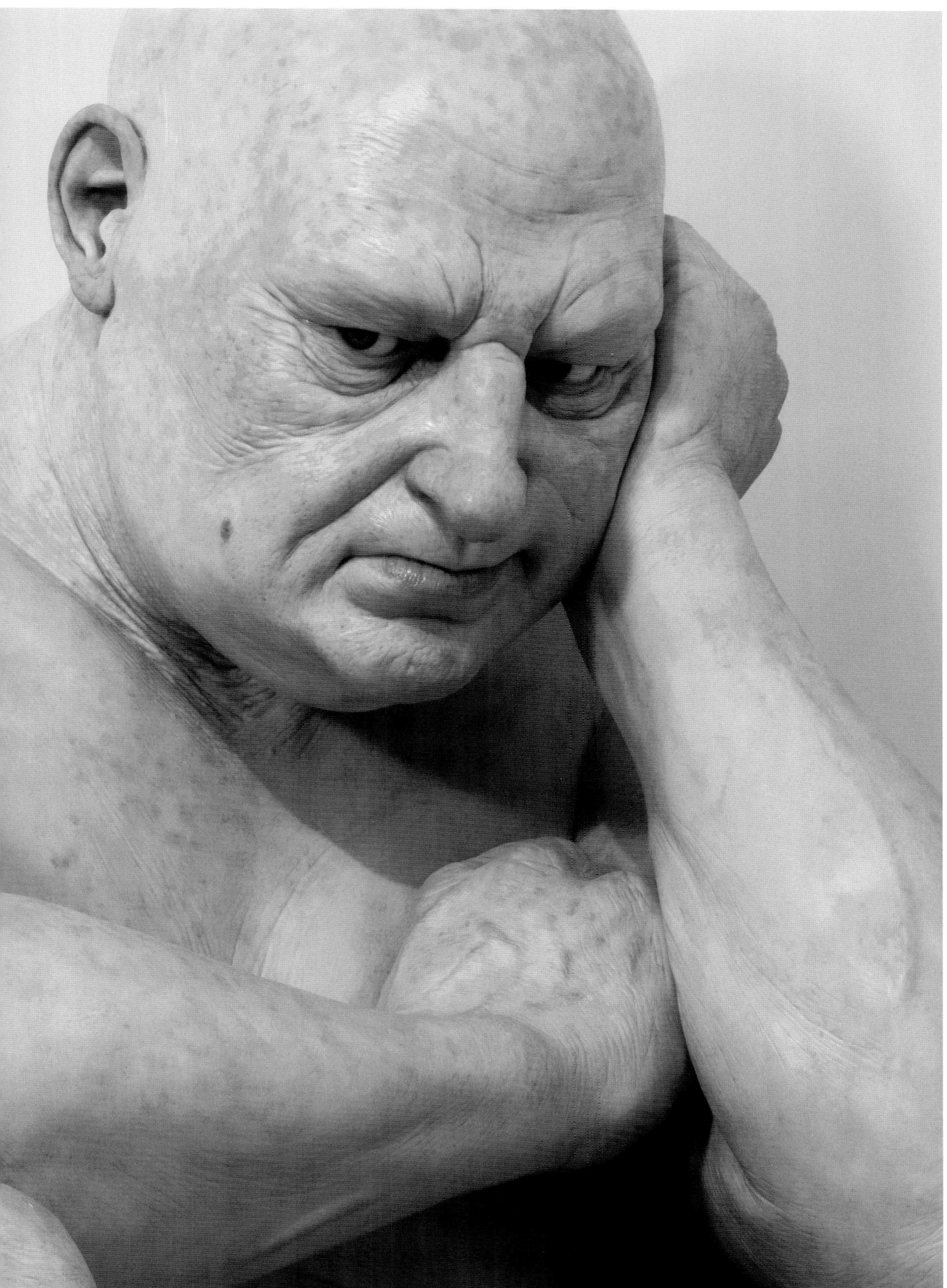

Old Woman in Bed 2000/2002
25 × 94 × 54 cm

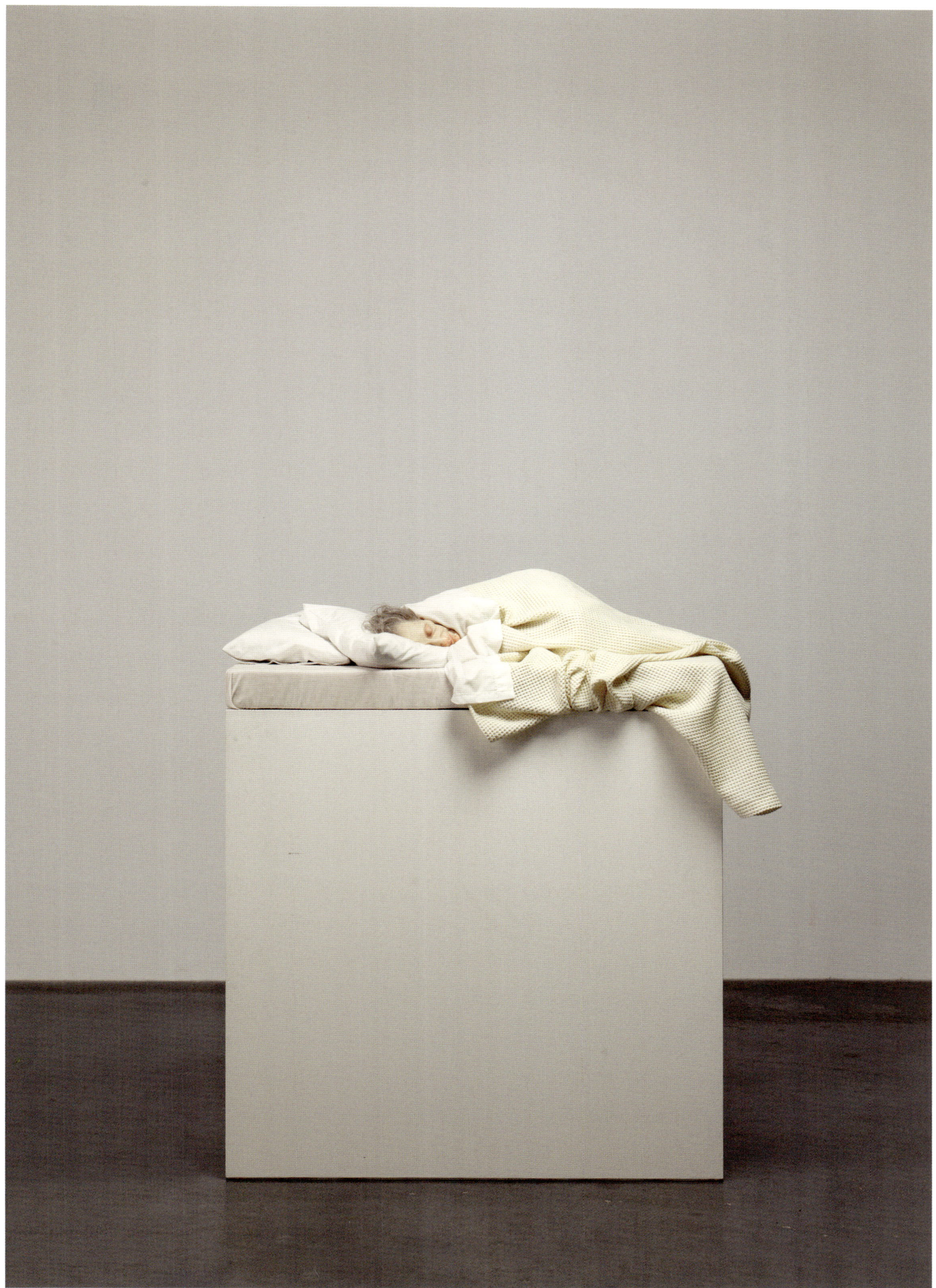

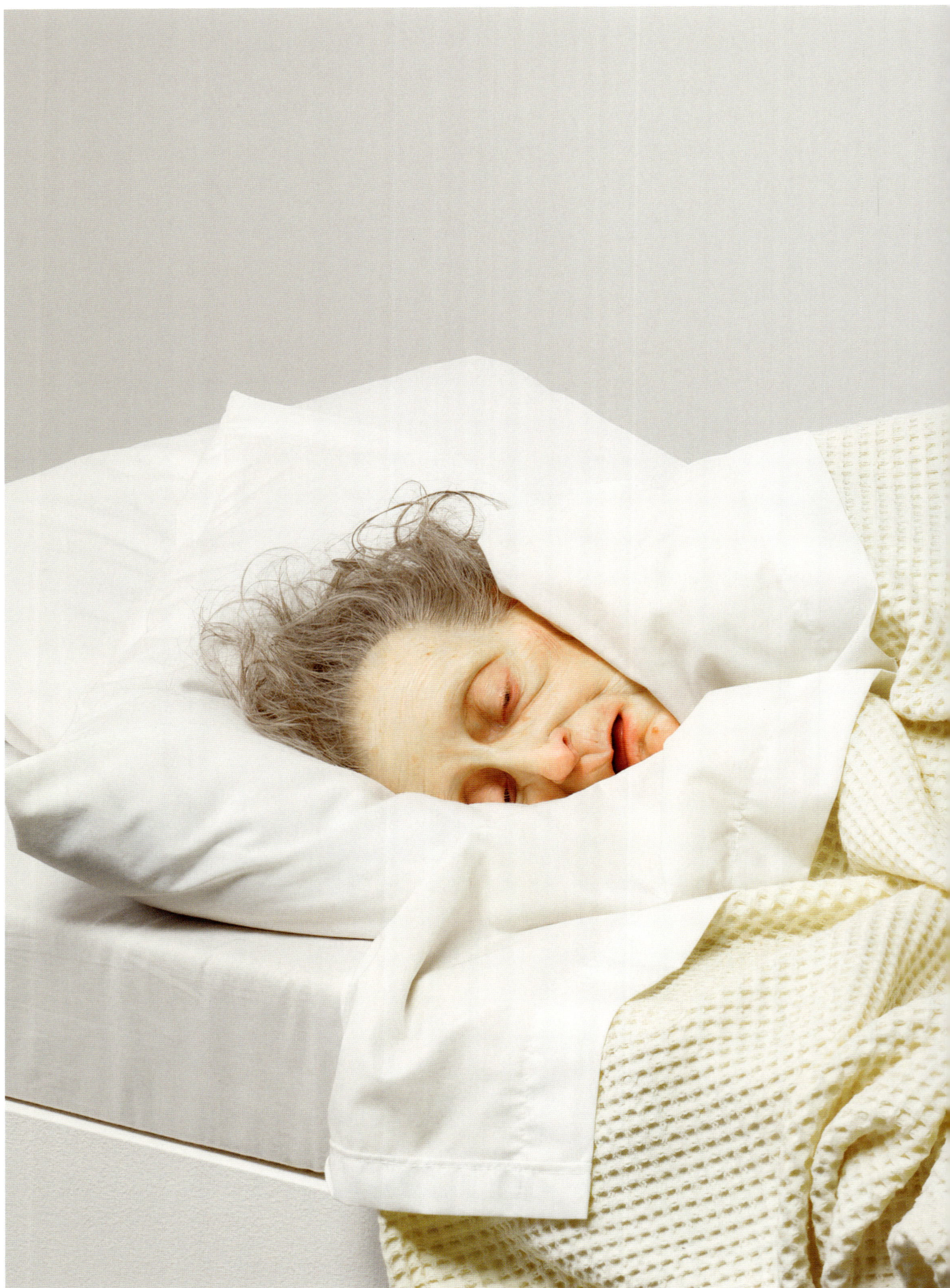

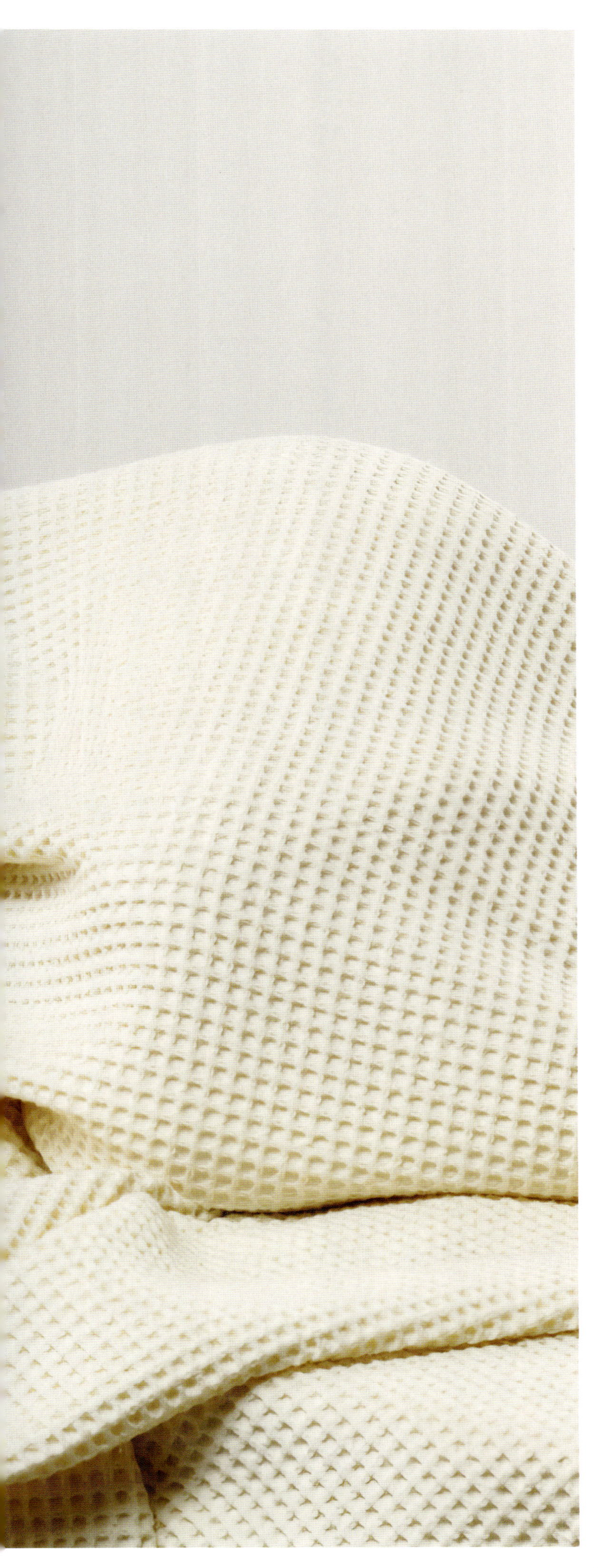

Pregnant Woman 2002
252 × 78 × 72 cm

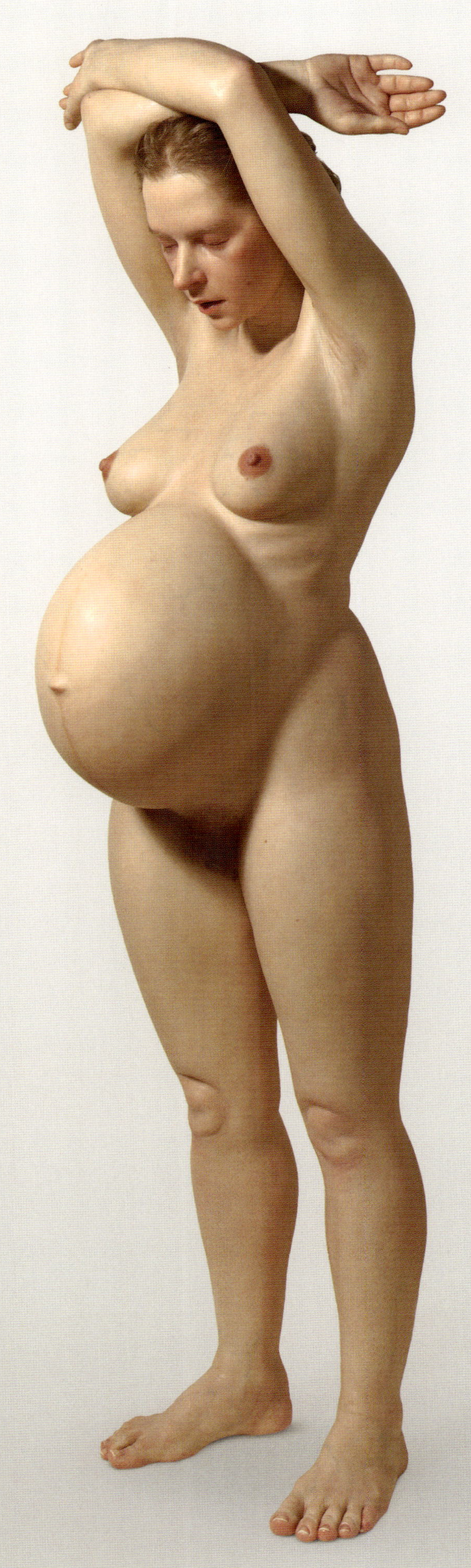

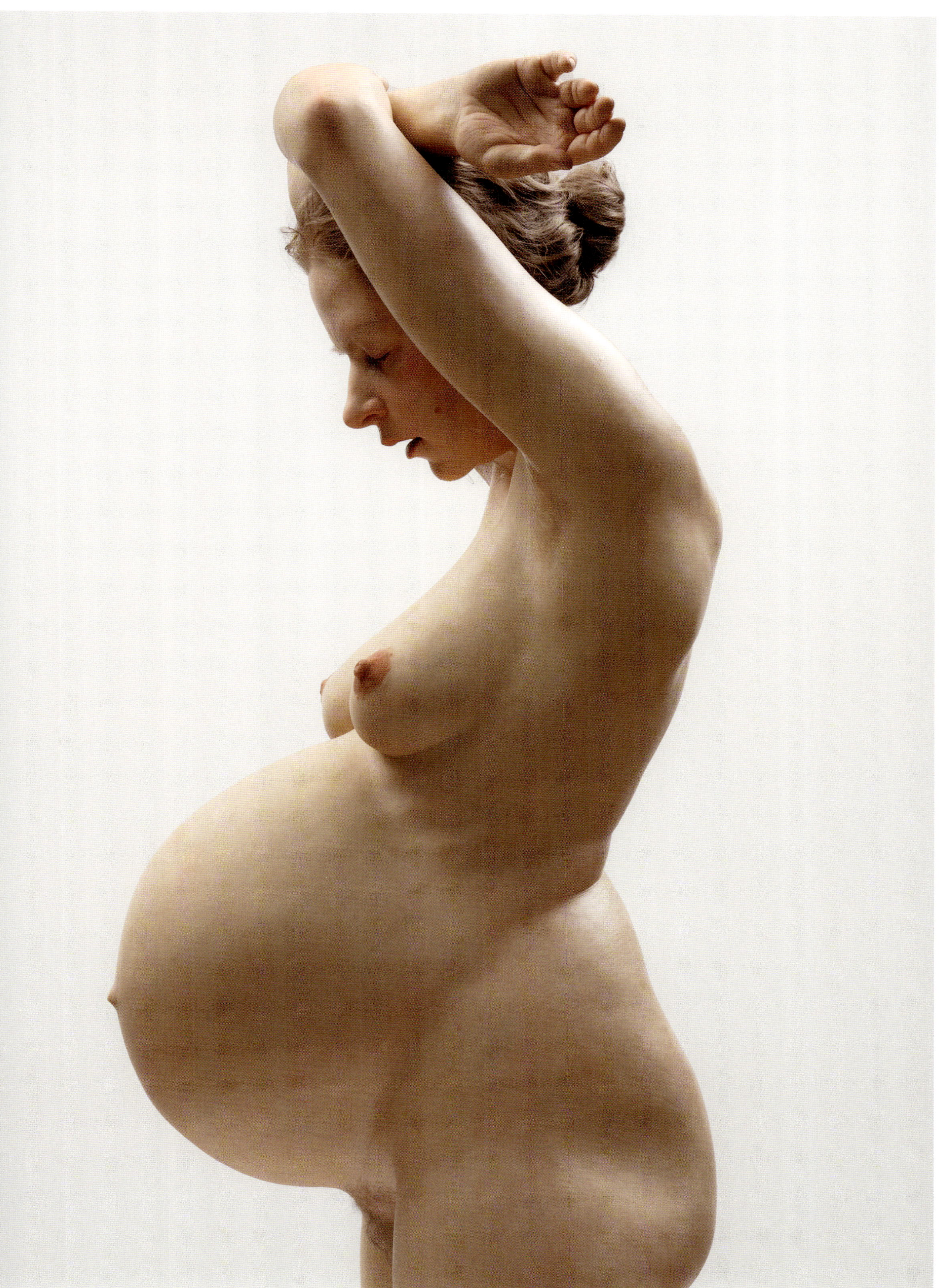

Spooning Couple 2005
14 × 65 × 35 cm

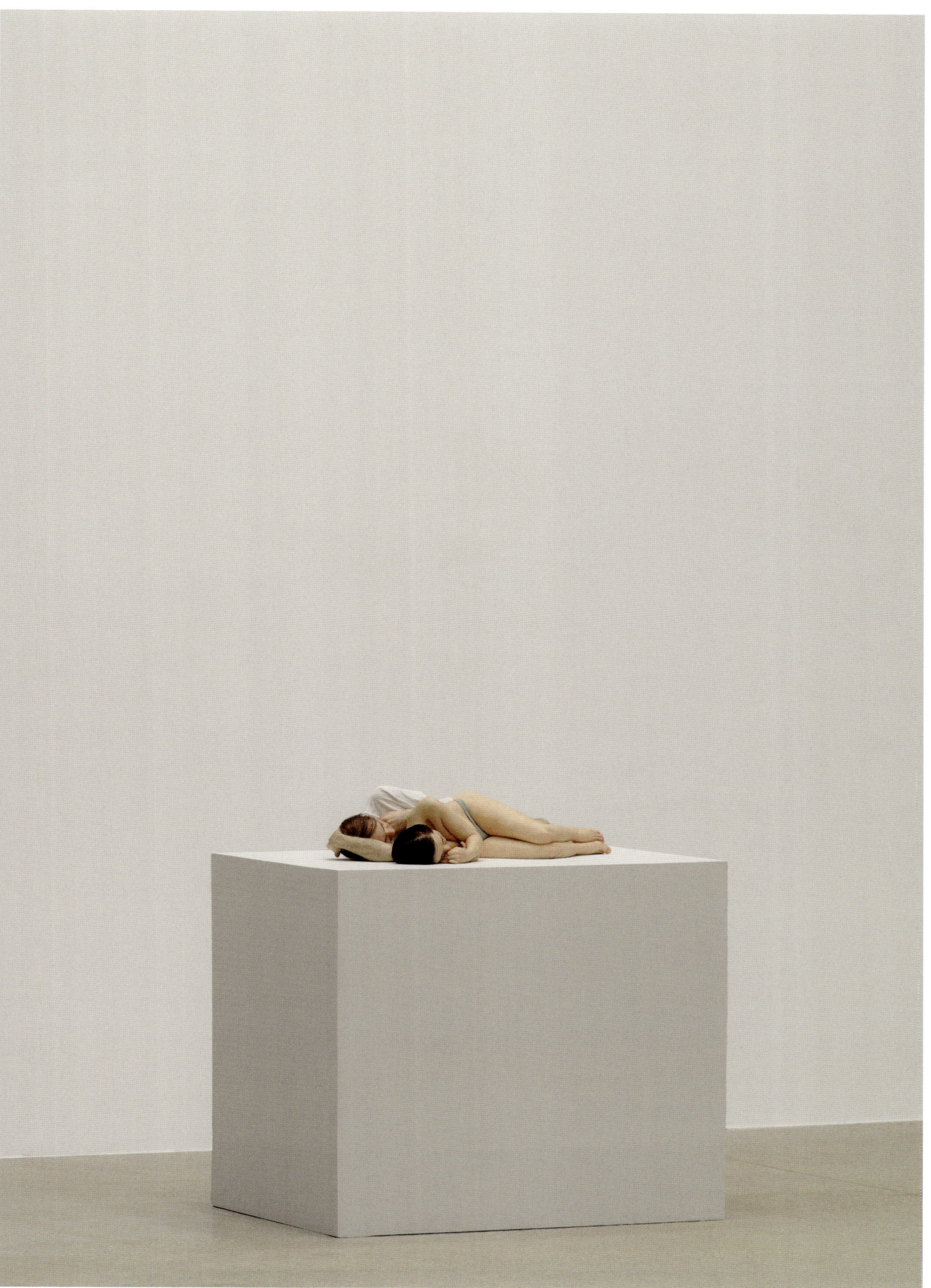

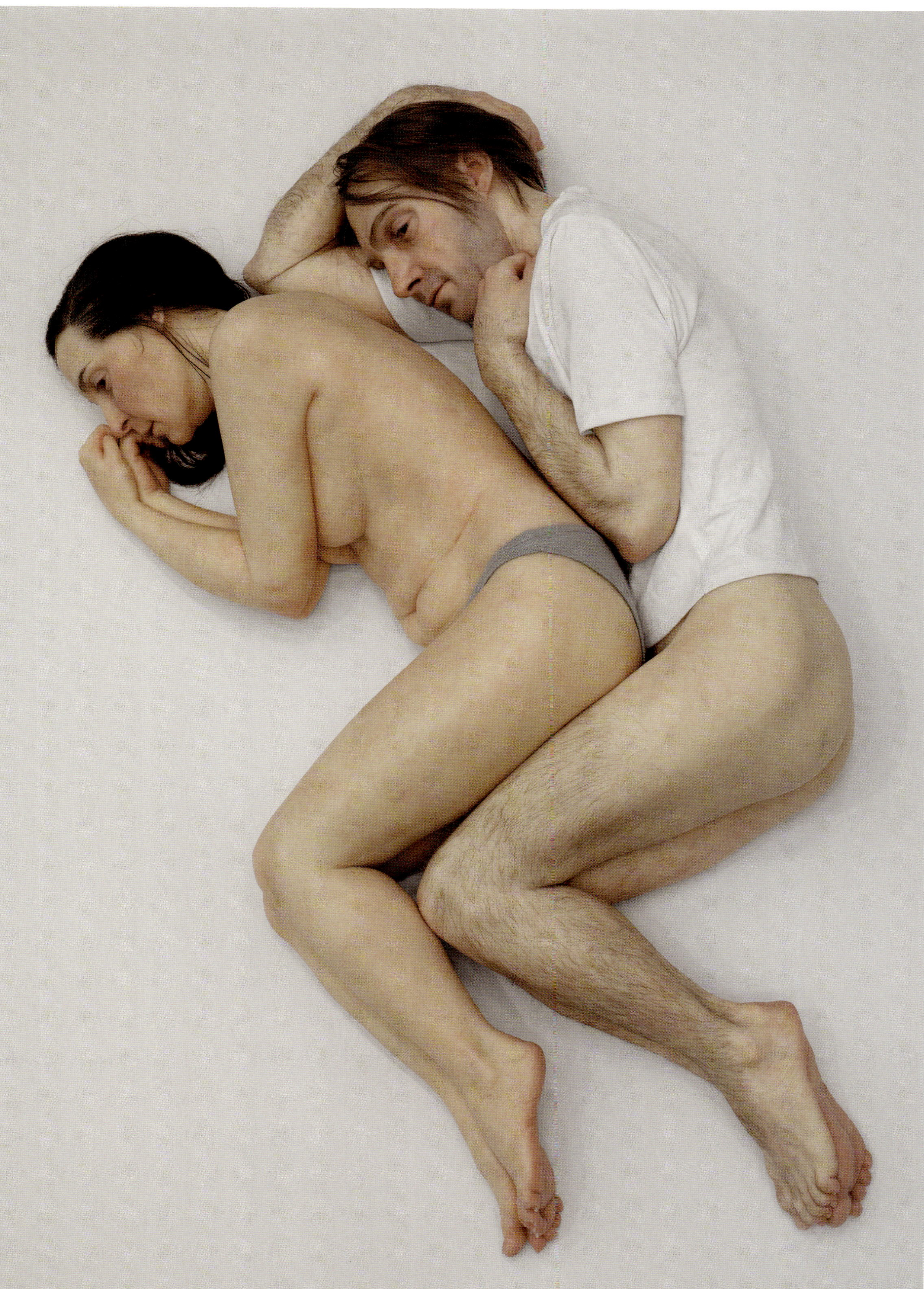

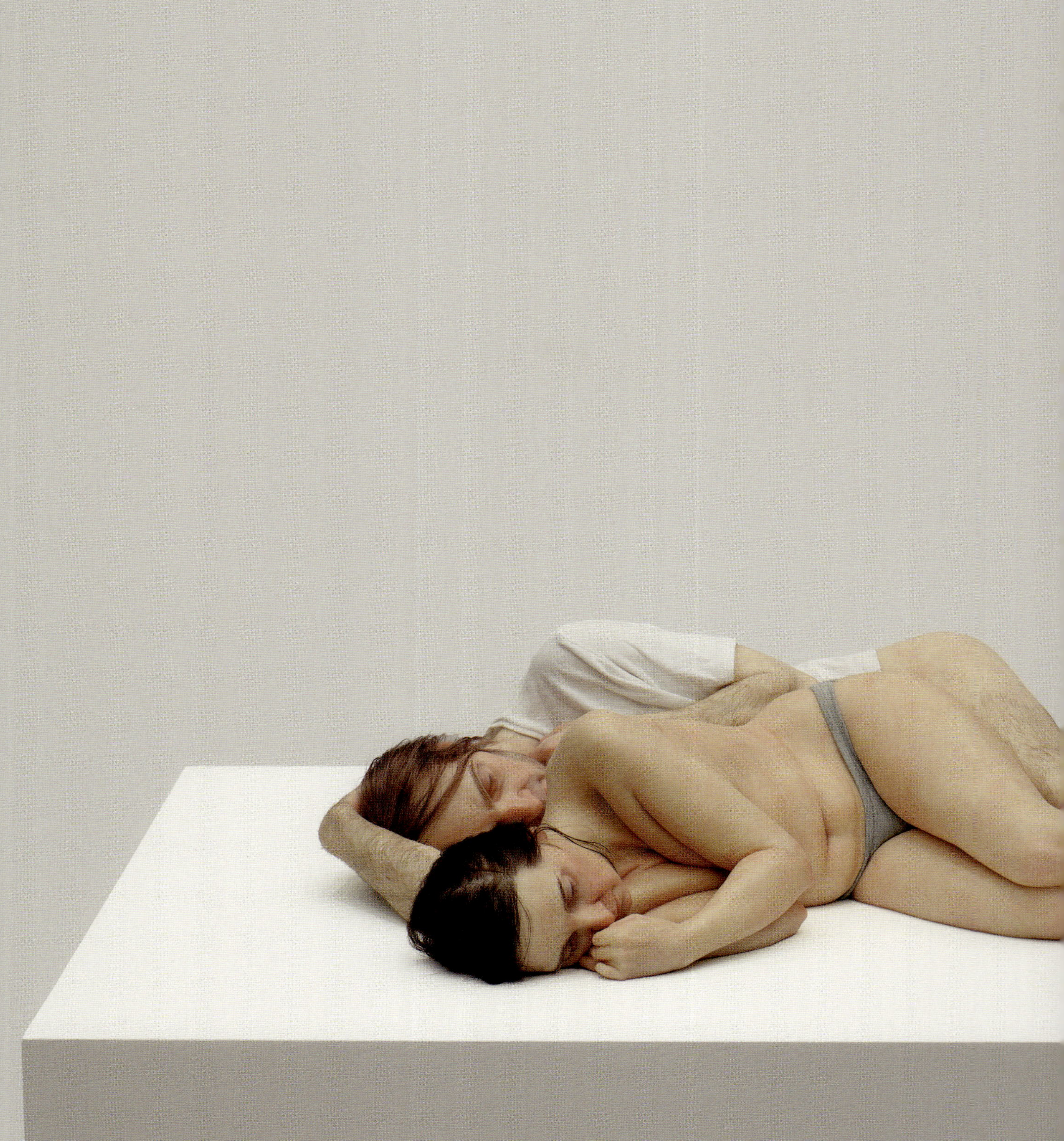

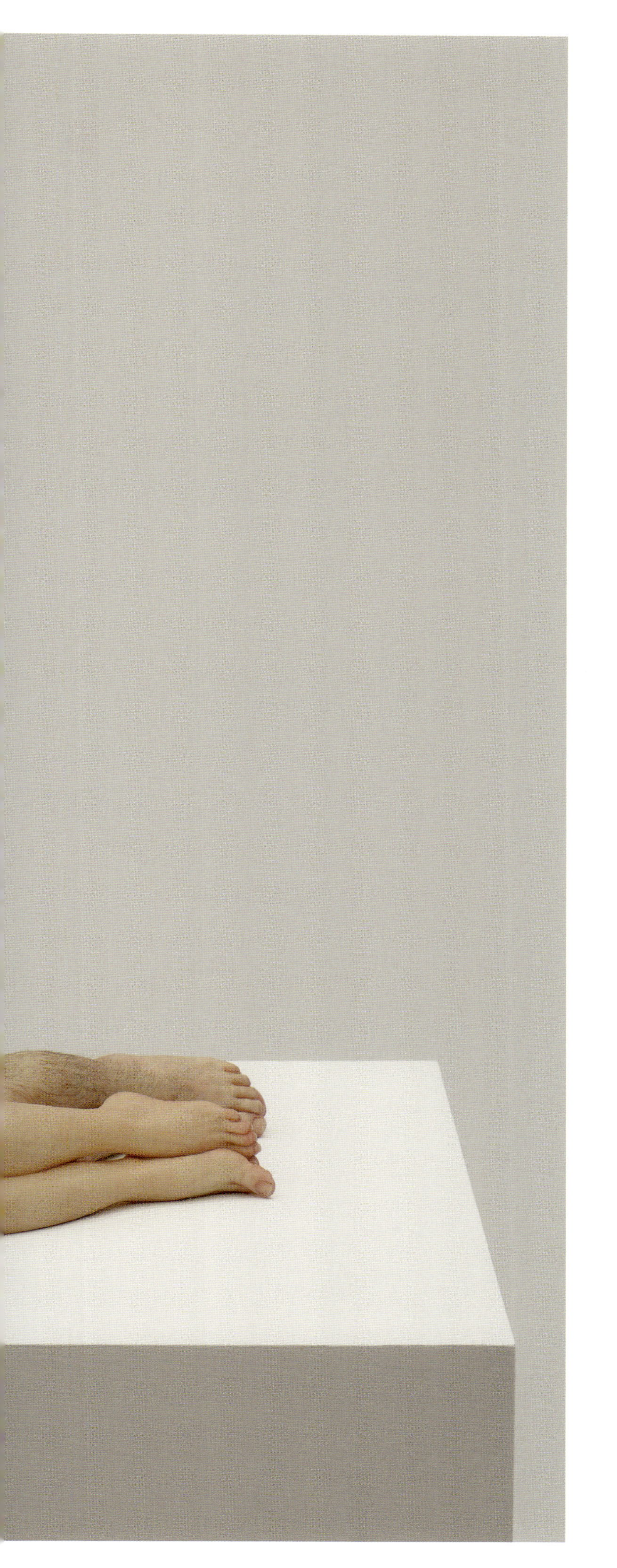

Woman with Sticks 2009–10
170 × 183 × 120 cm

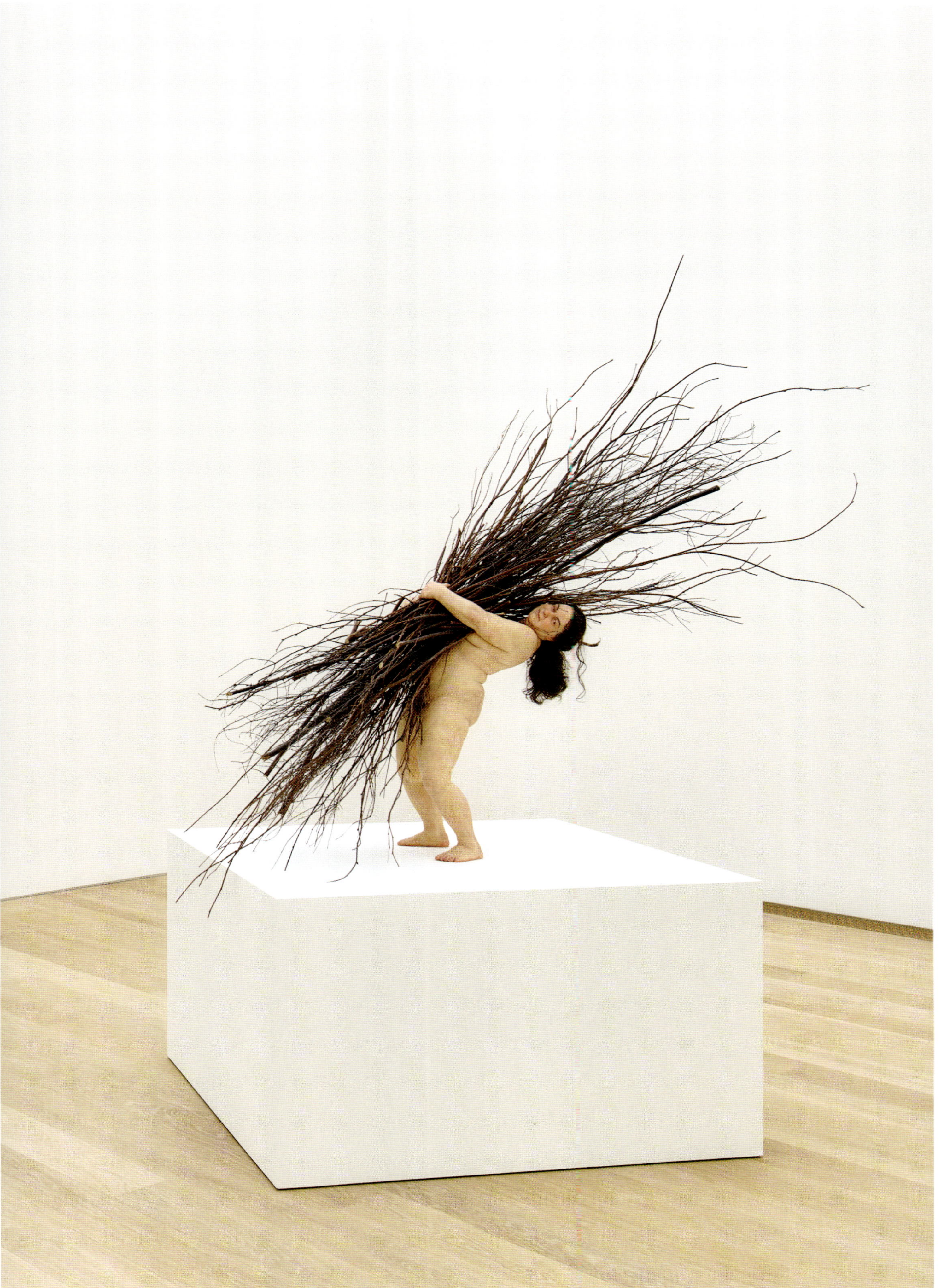

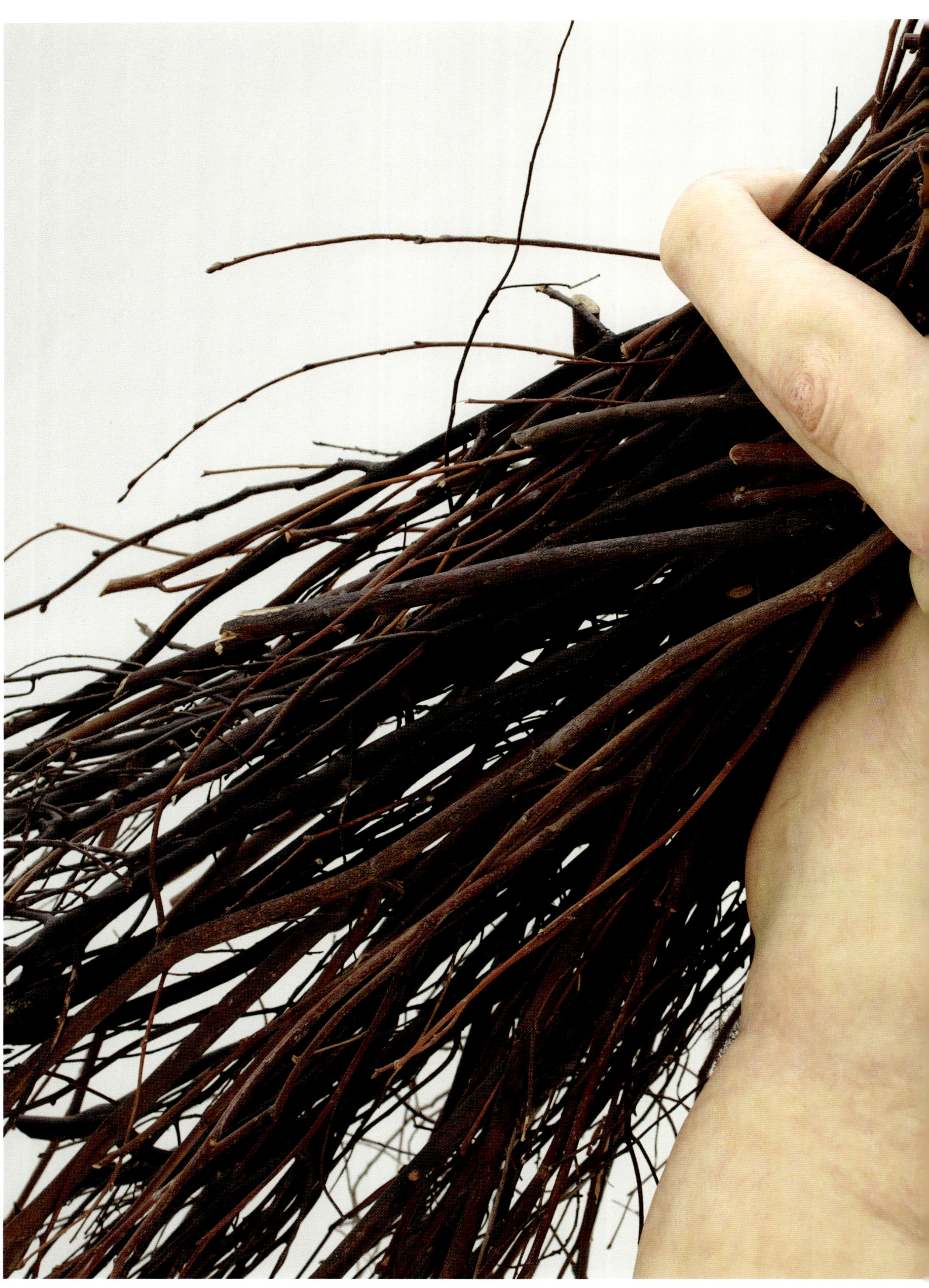

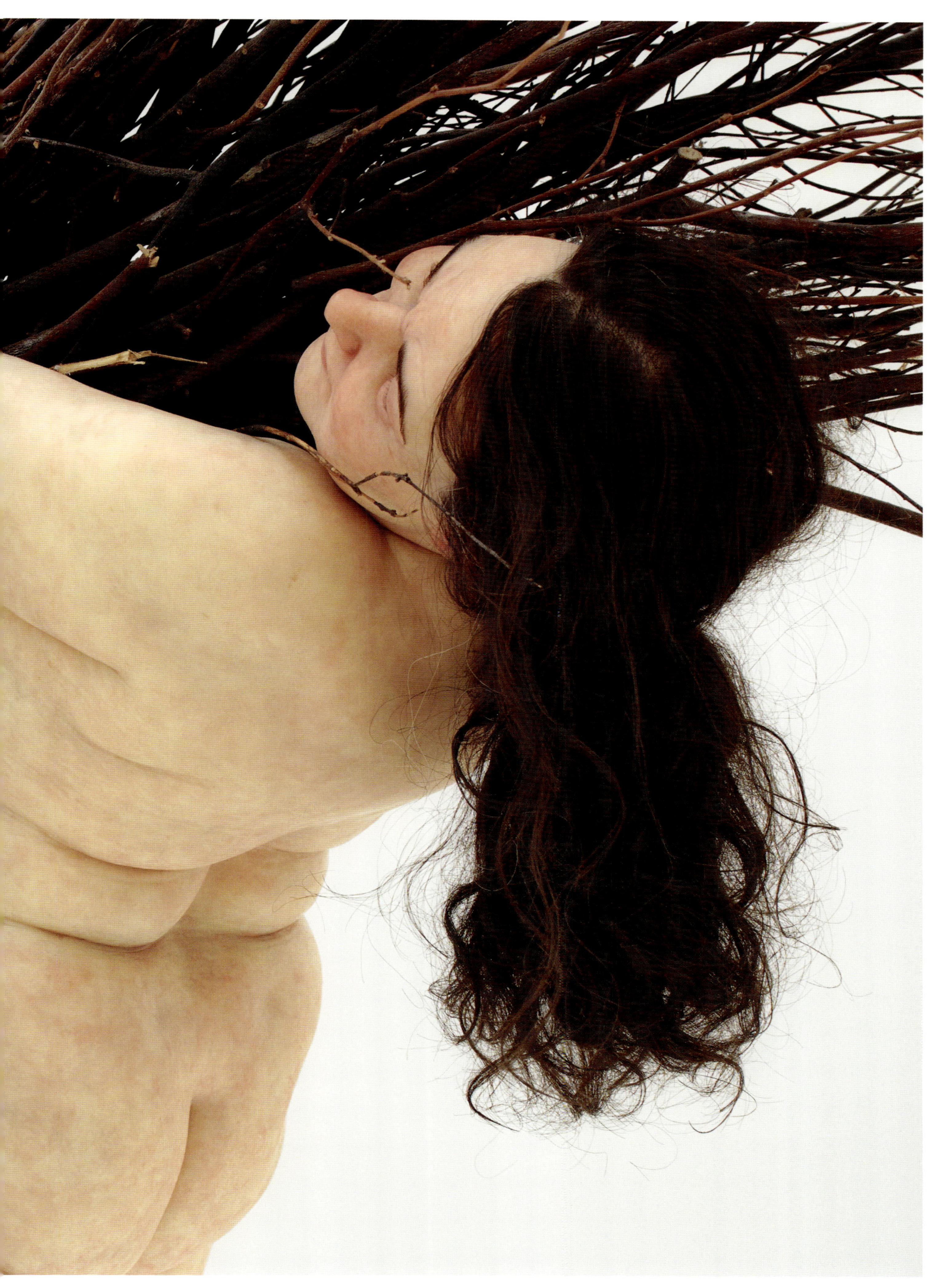

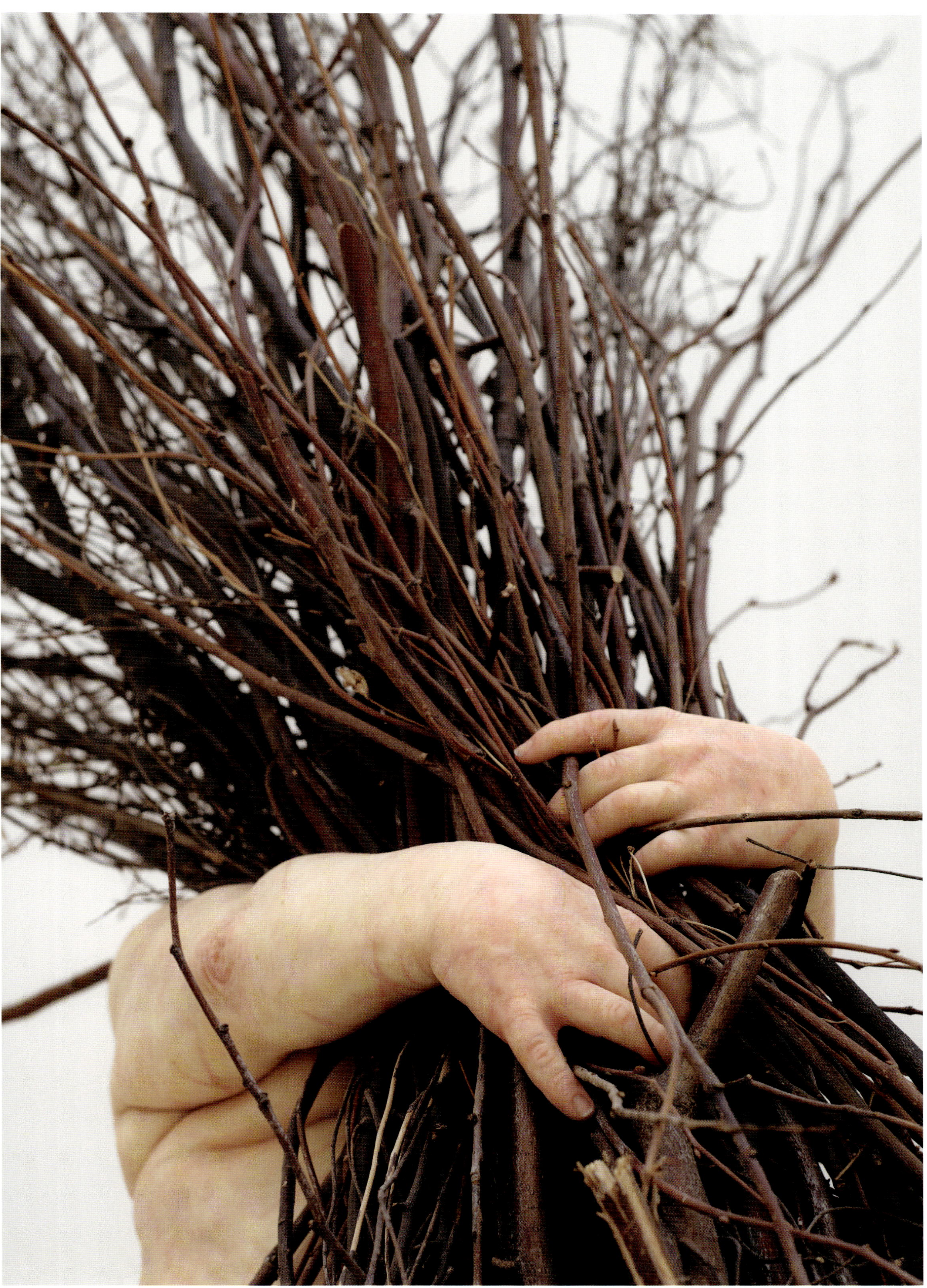

Couple Under an Umbrella 2013
275 × 455 × 330 cm

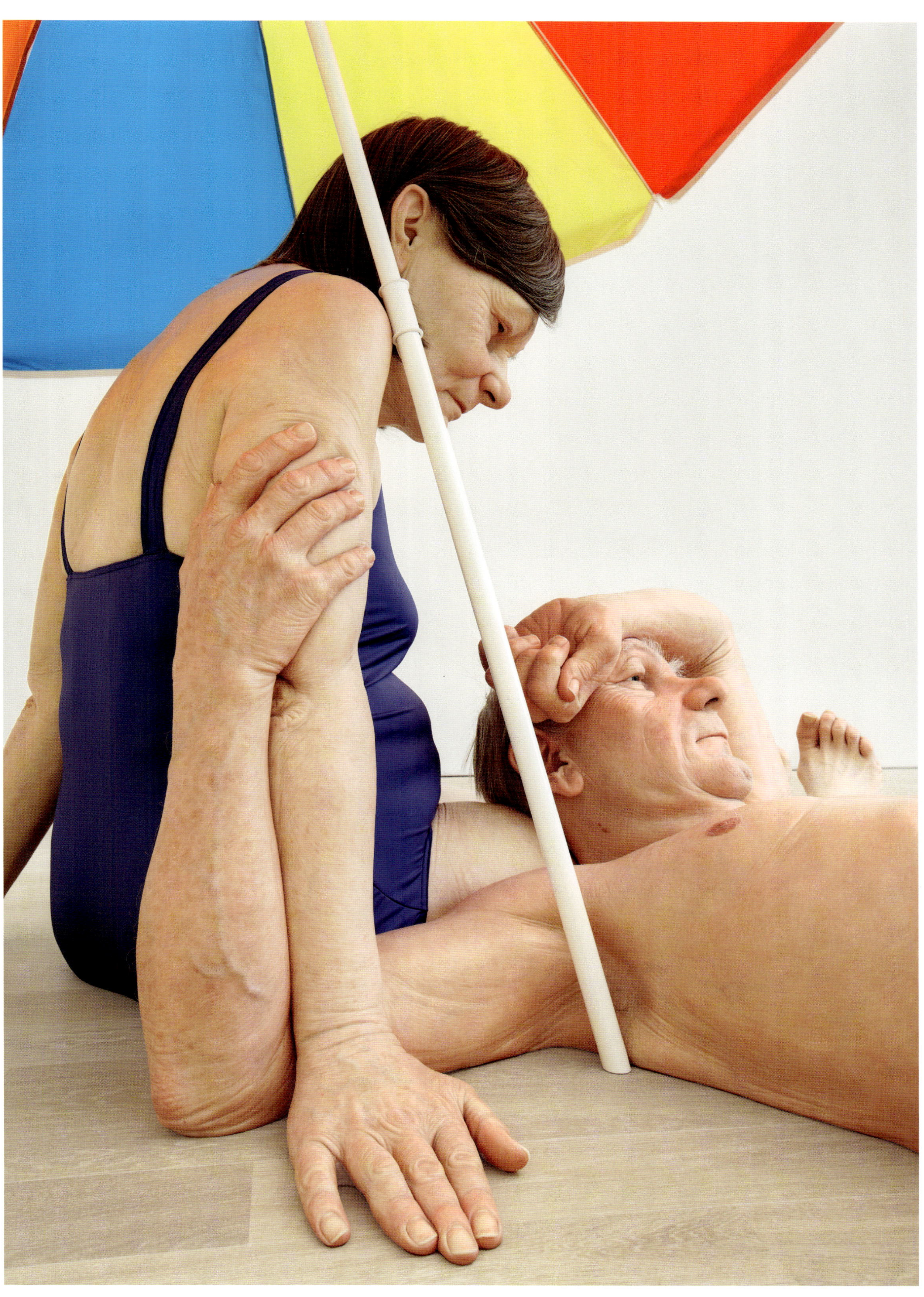

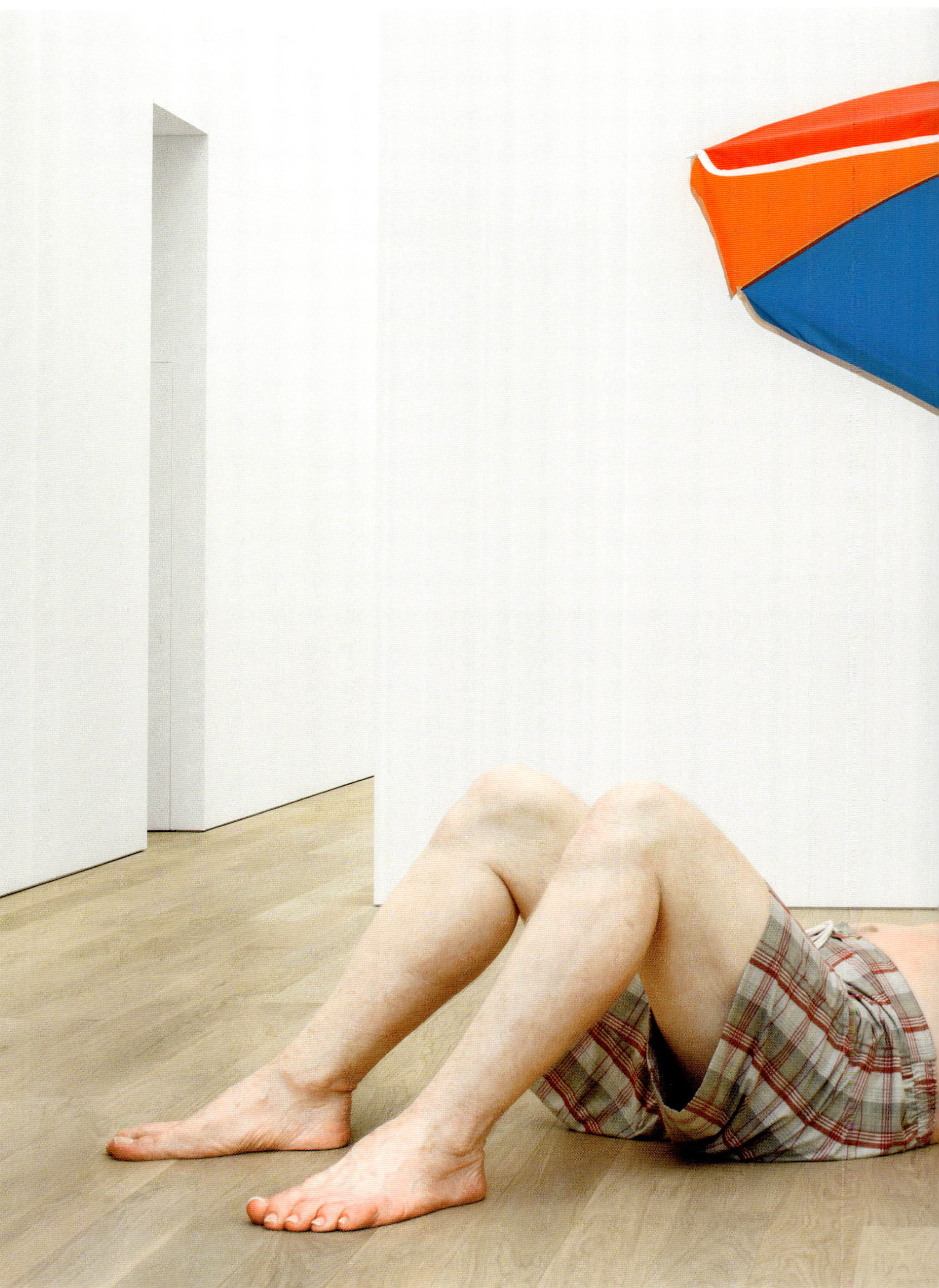

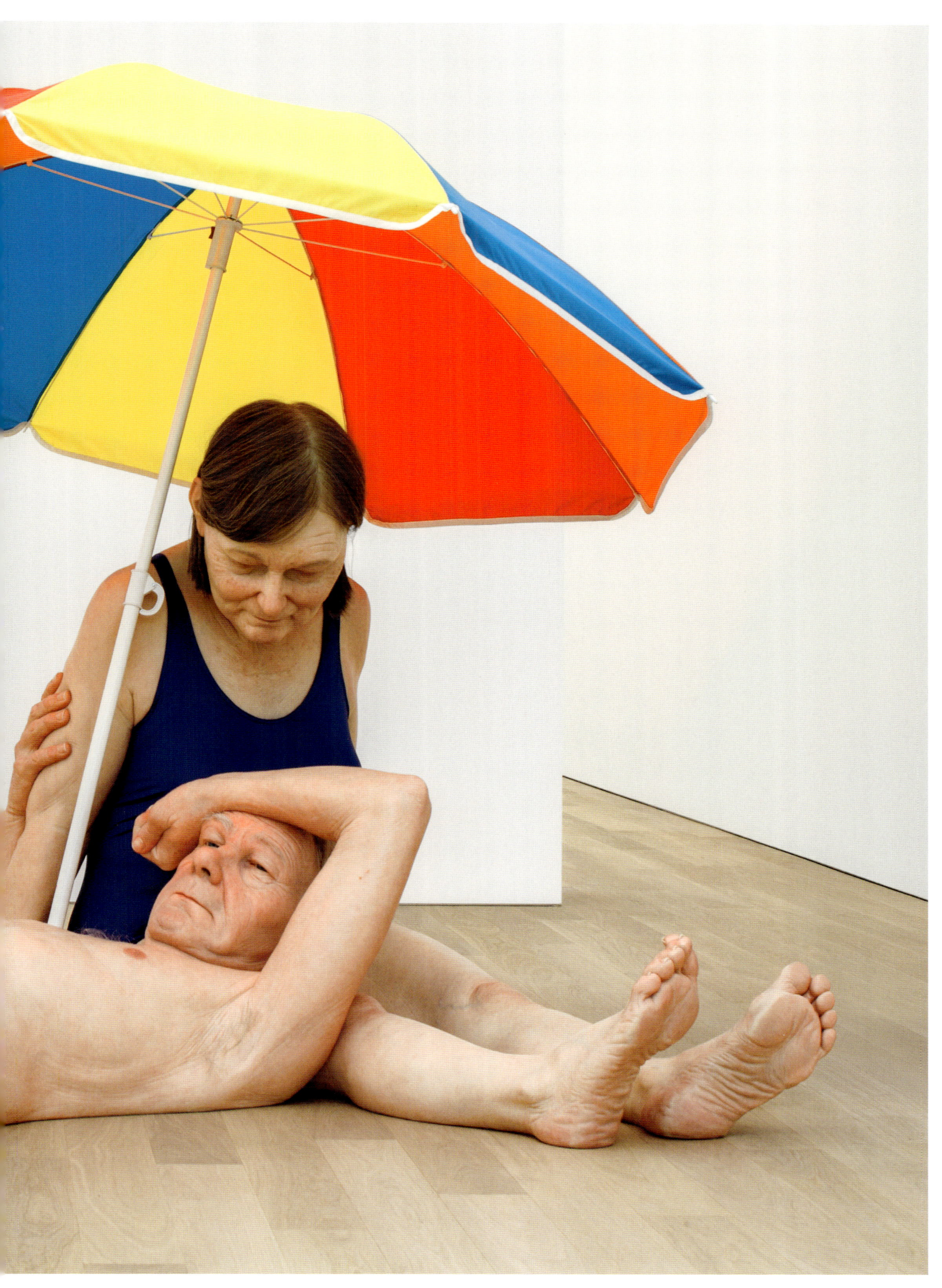

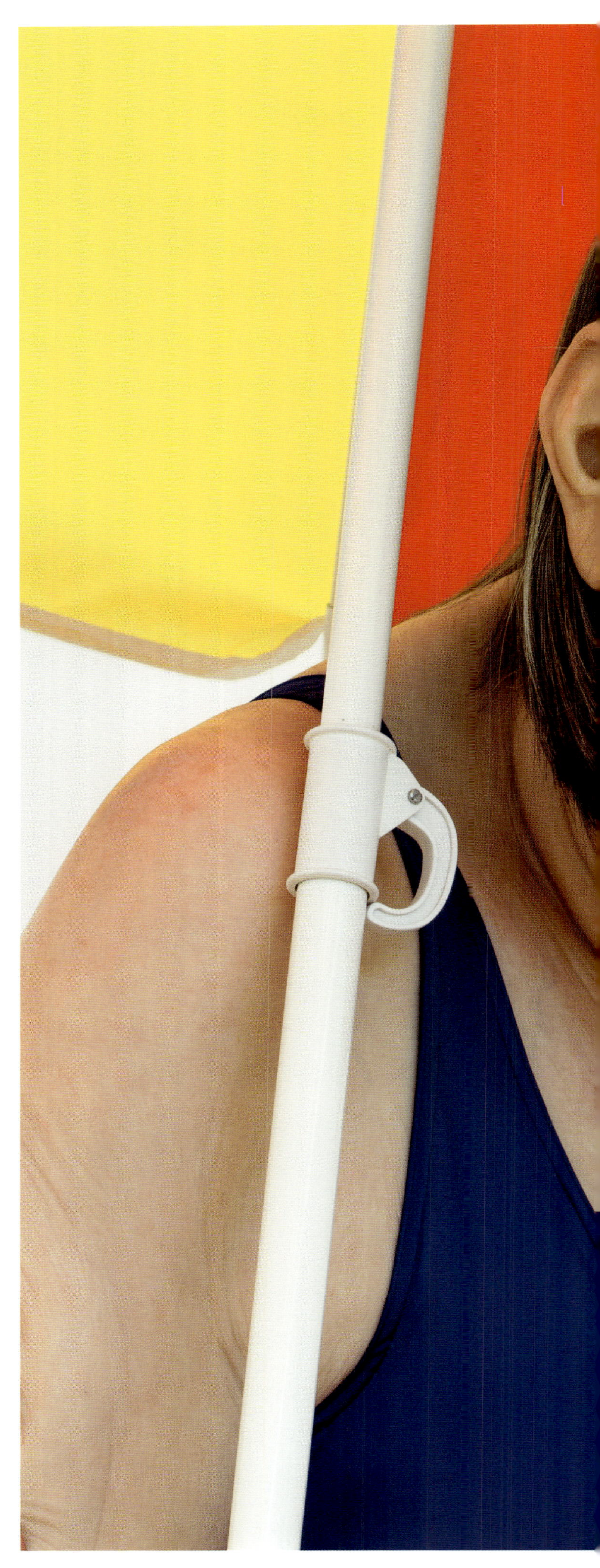

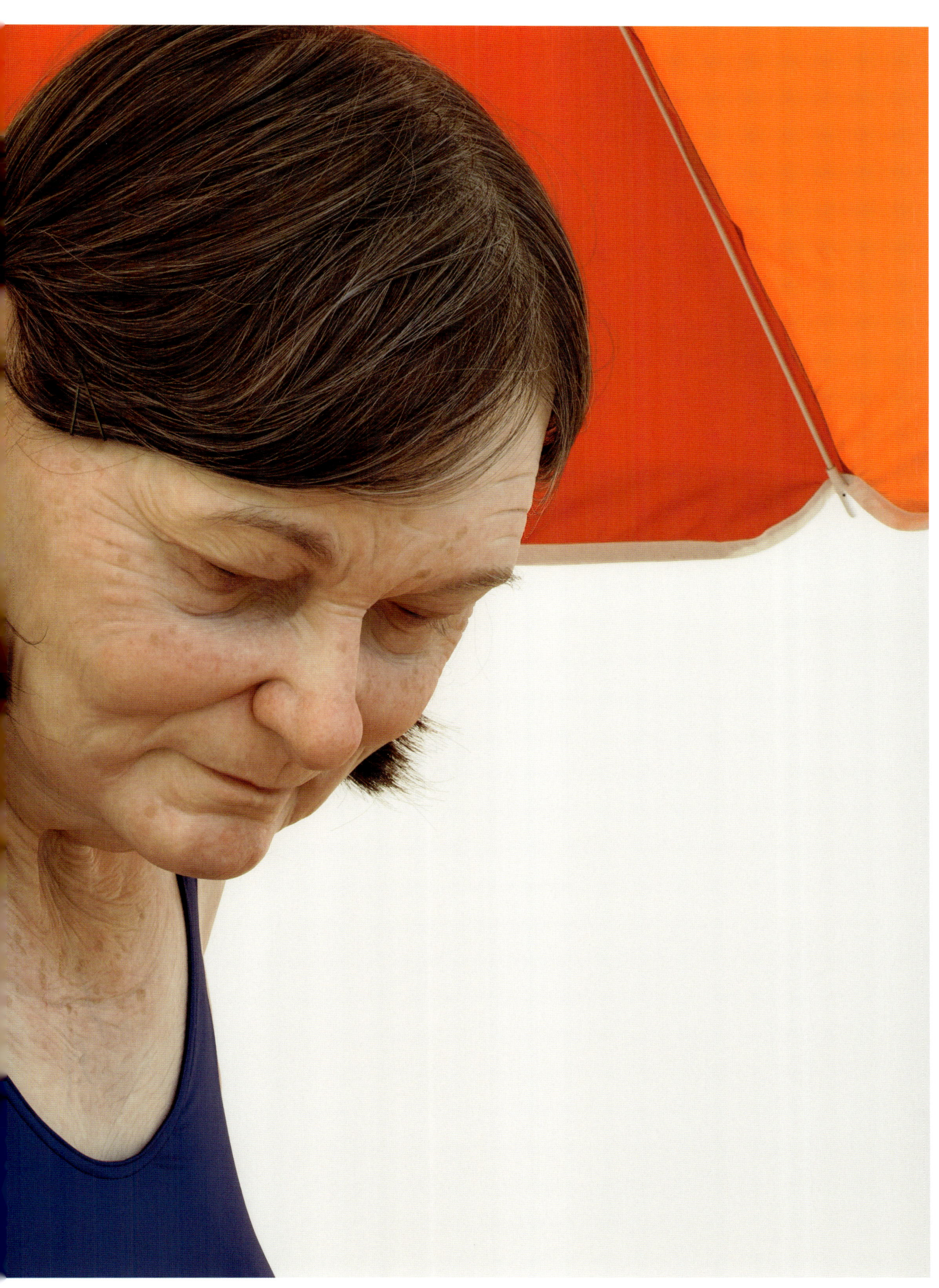

Woman with Shopping 2013
113 × 46 × 30 cm

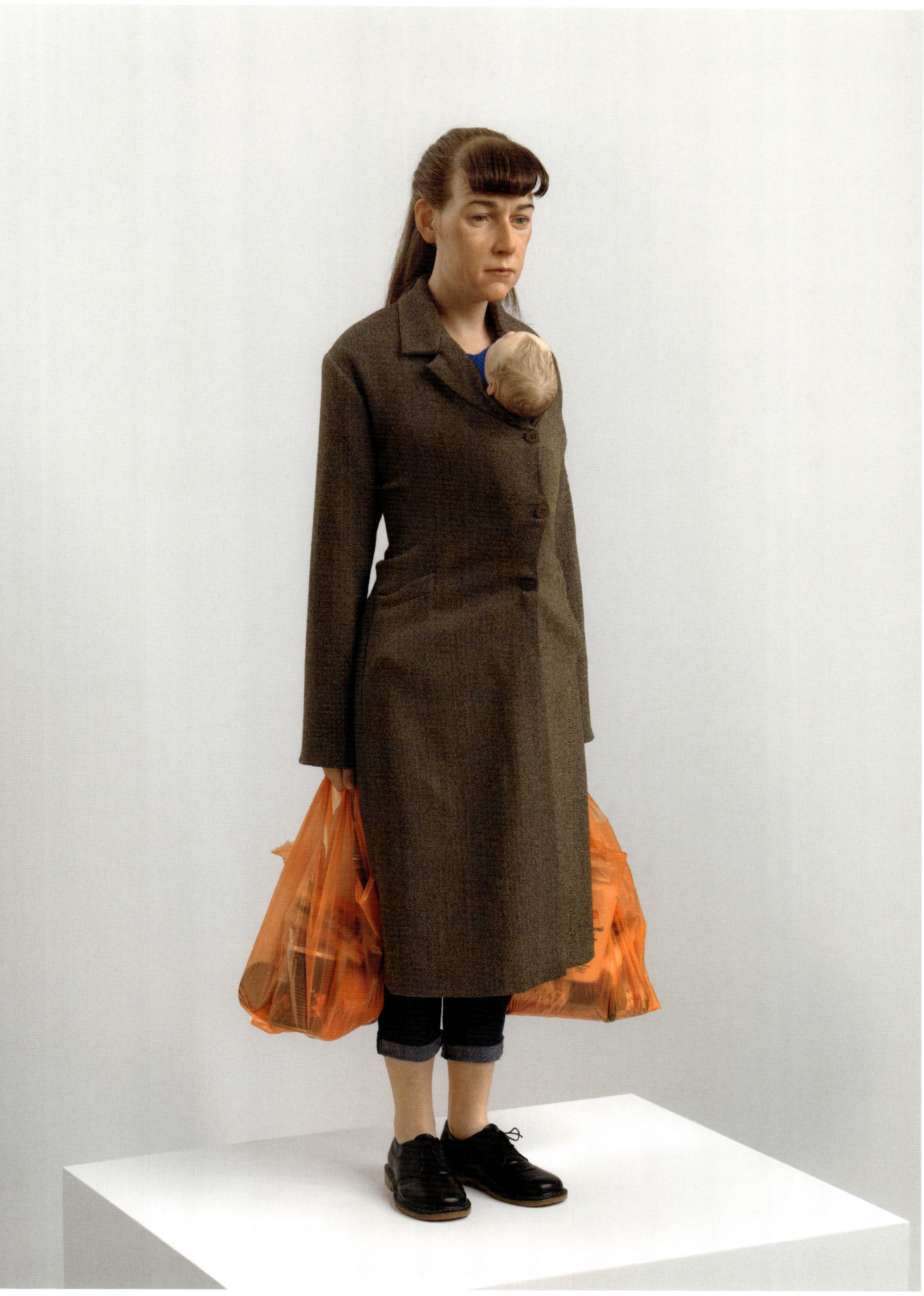

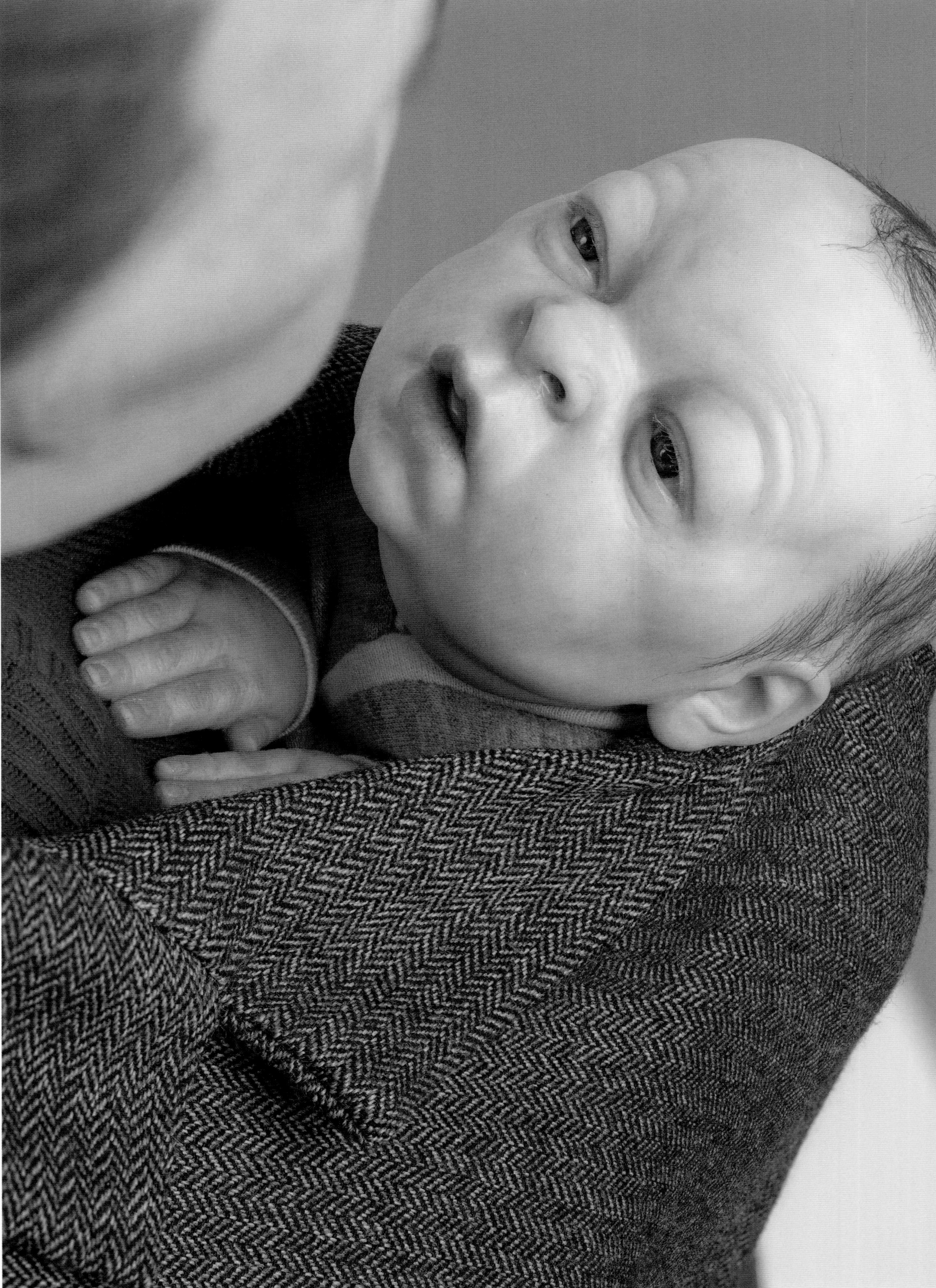

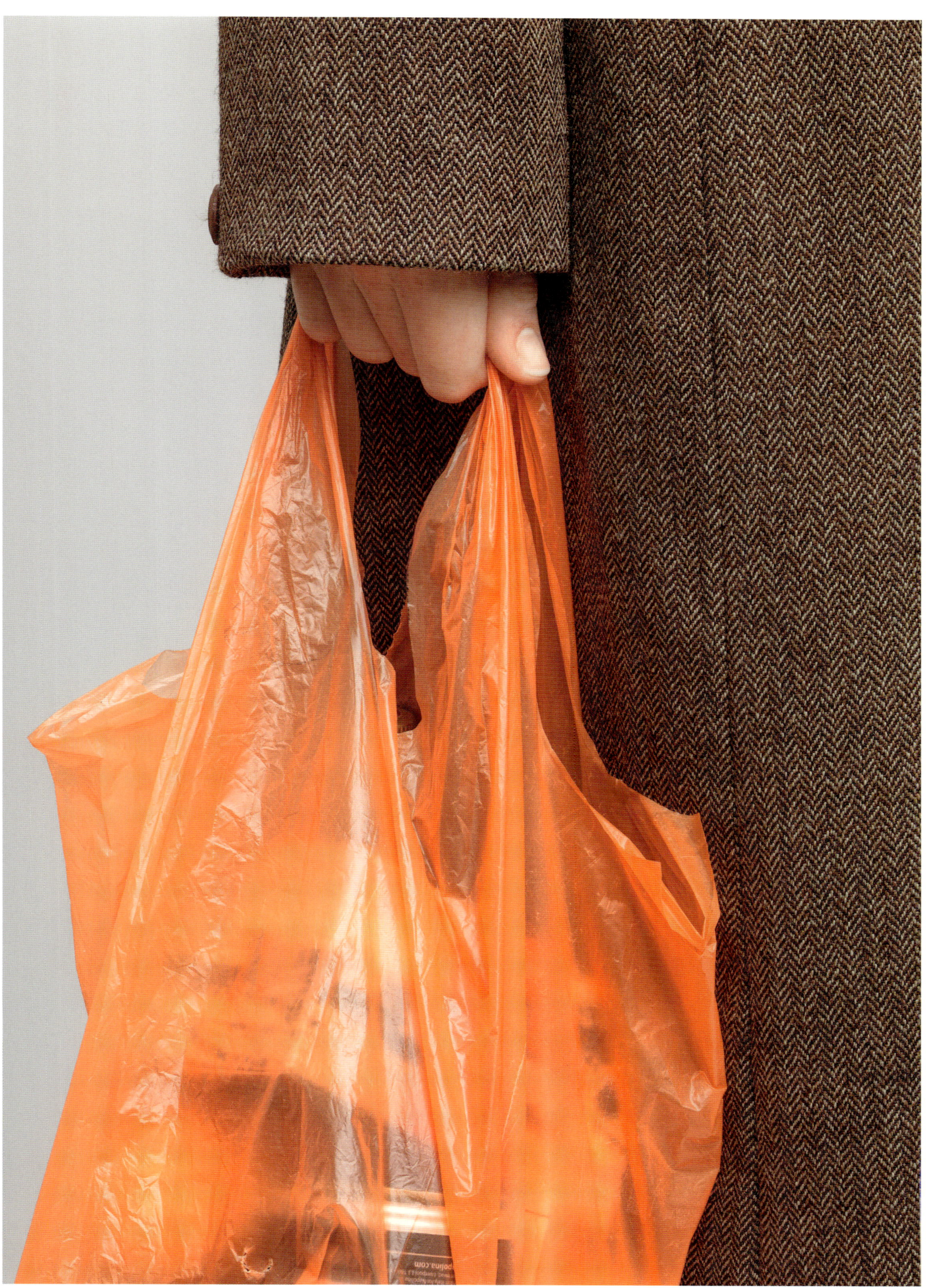

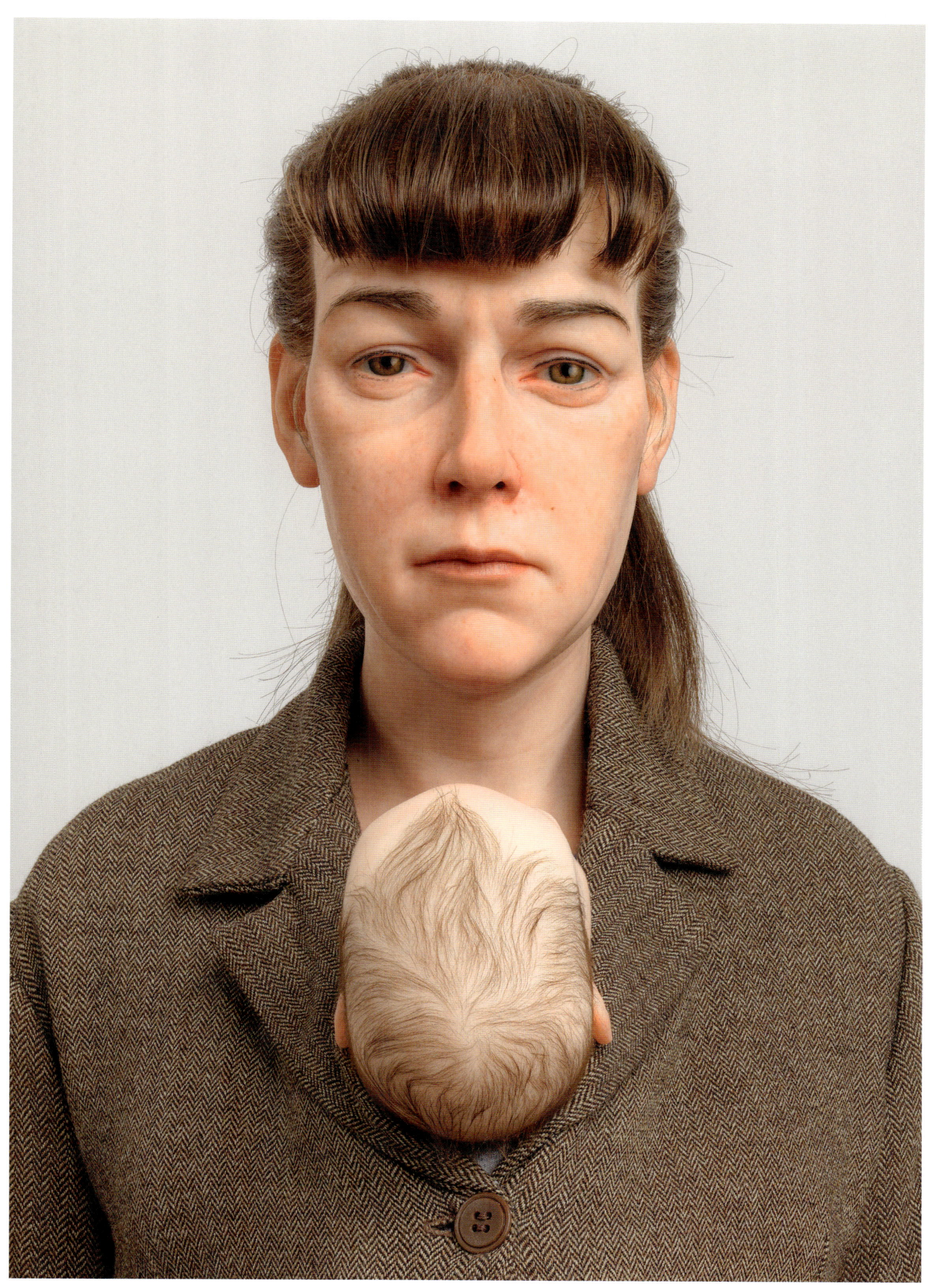

Young Couple 2013
89 × 43 × 23 cm

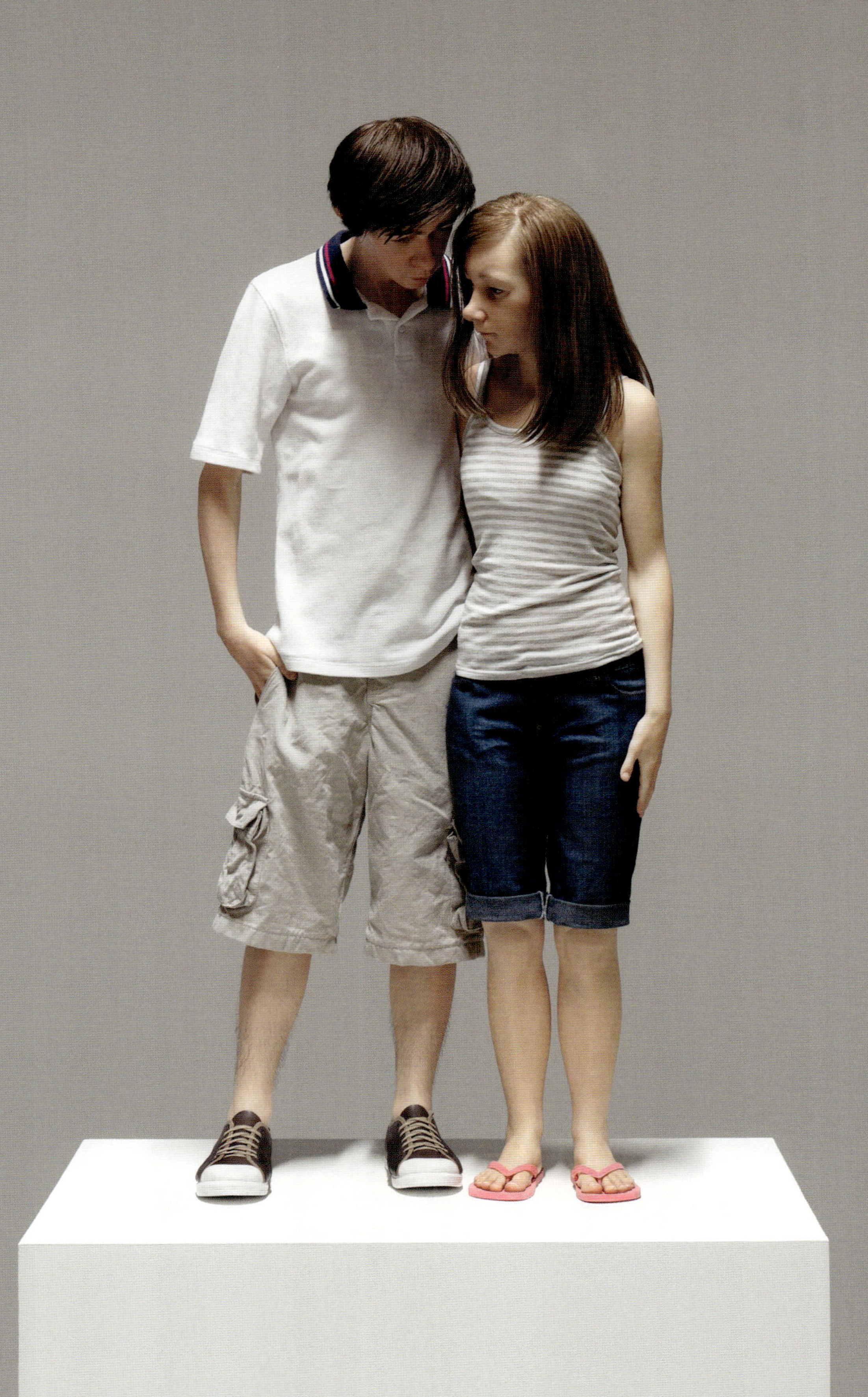

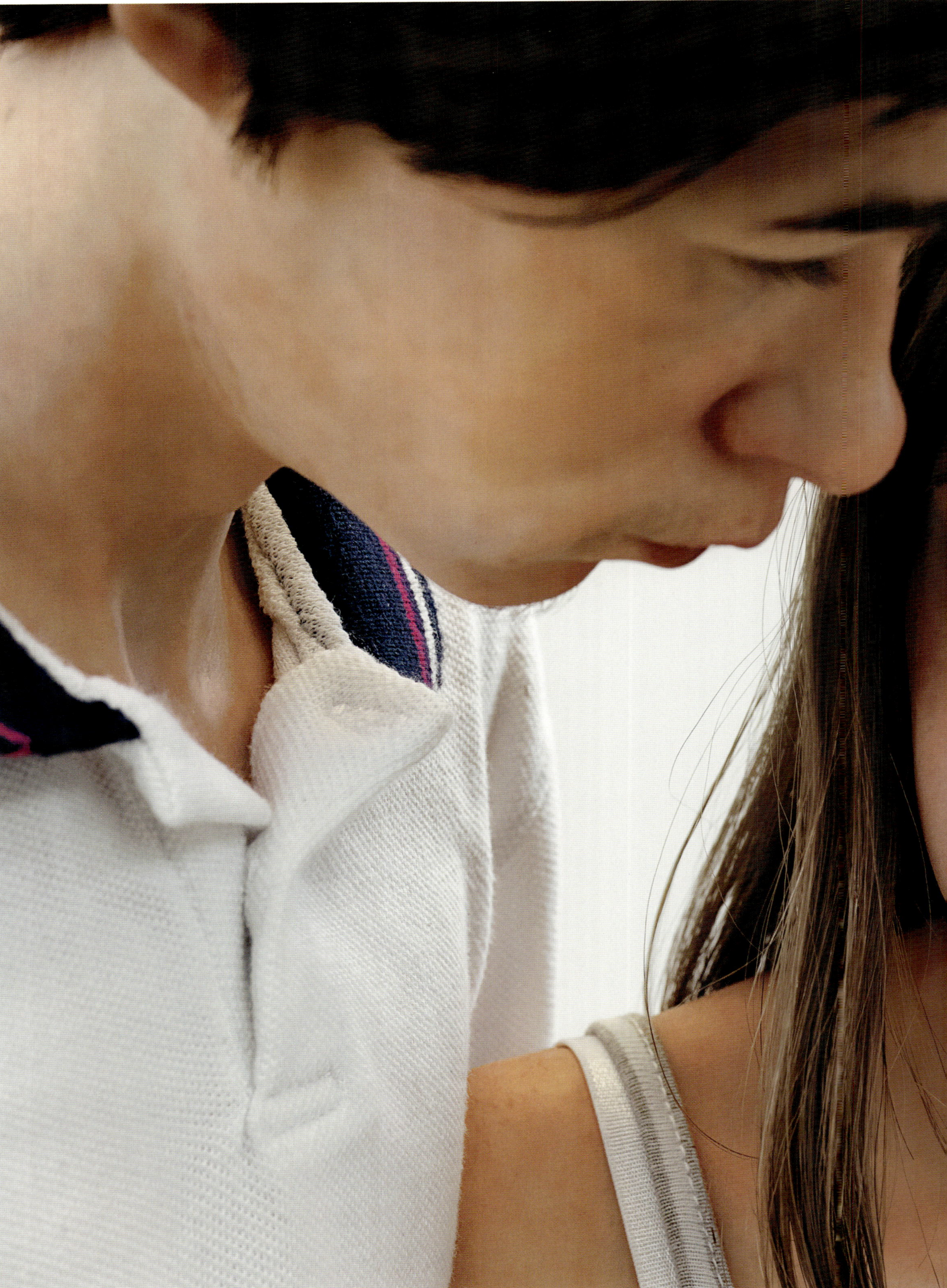

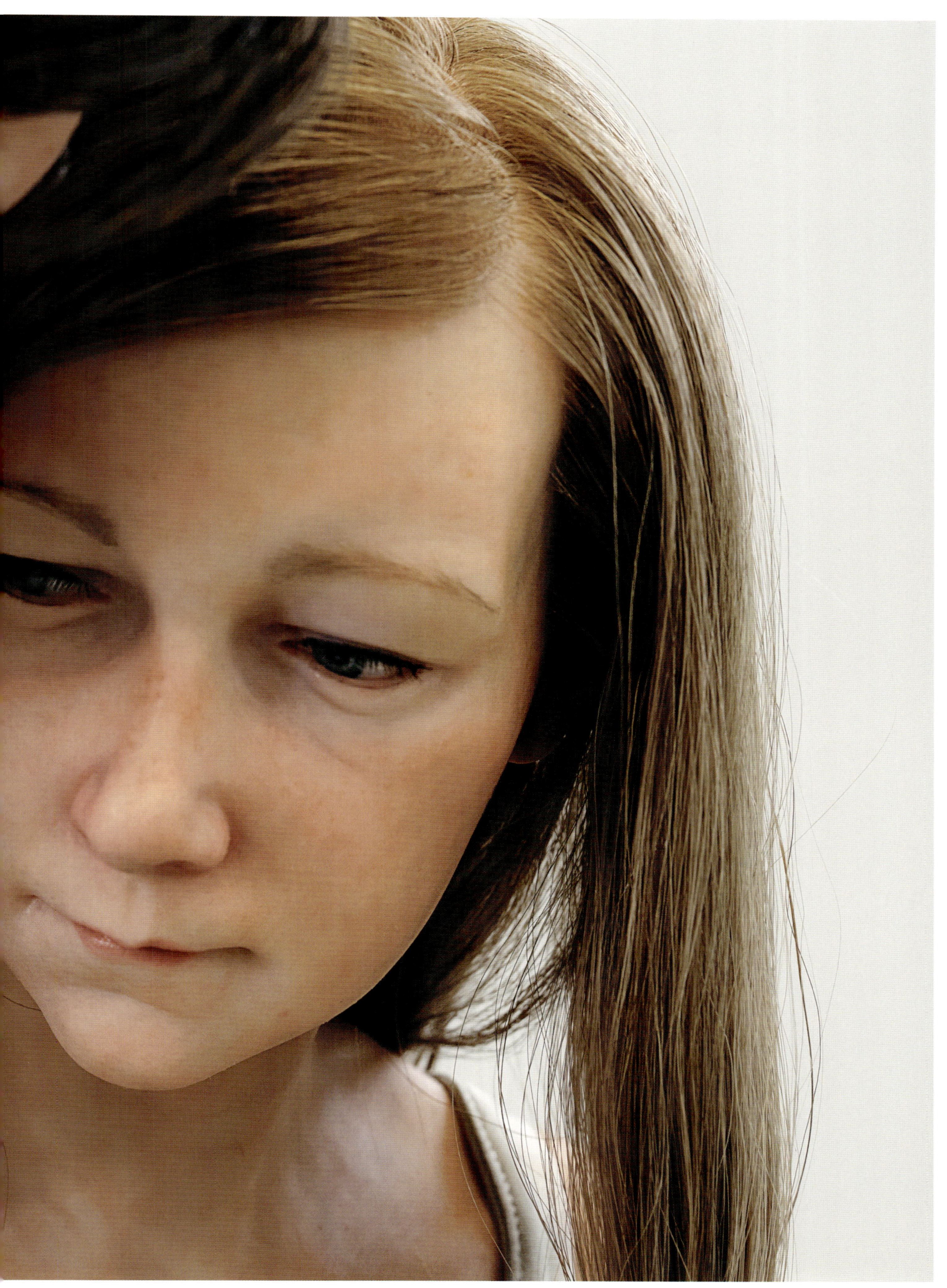

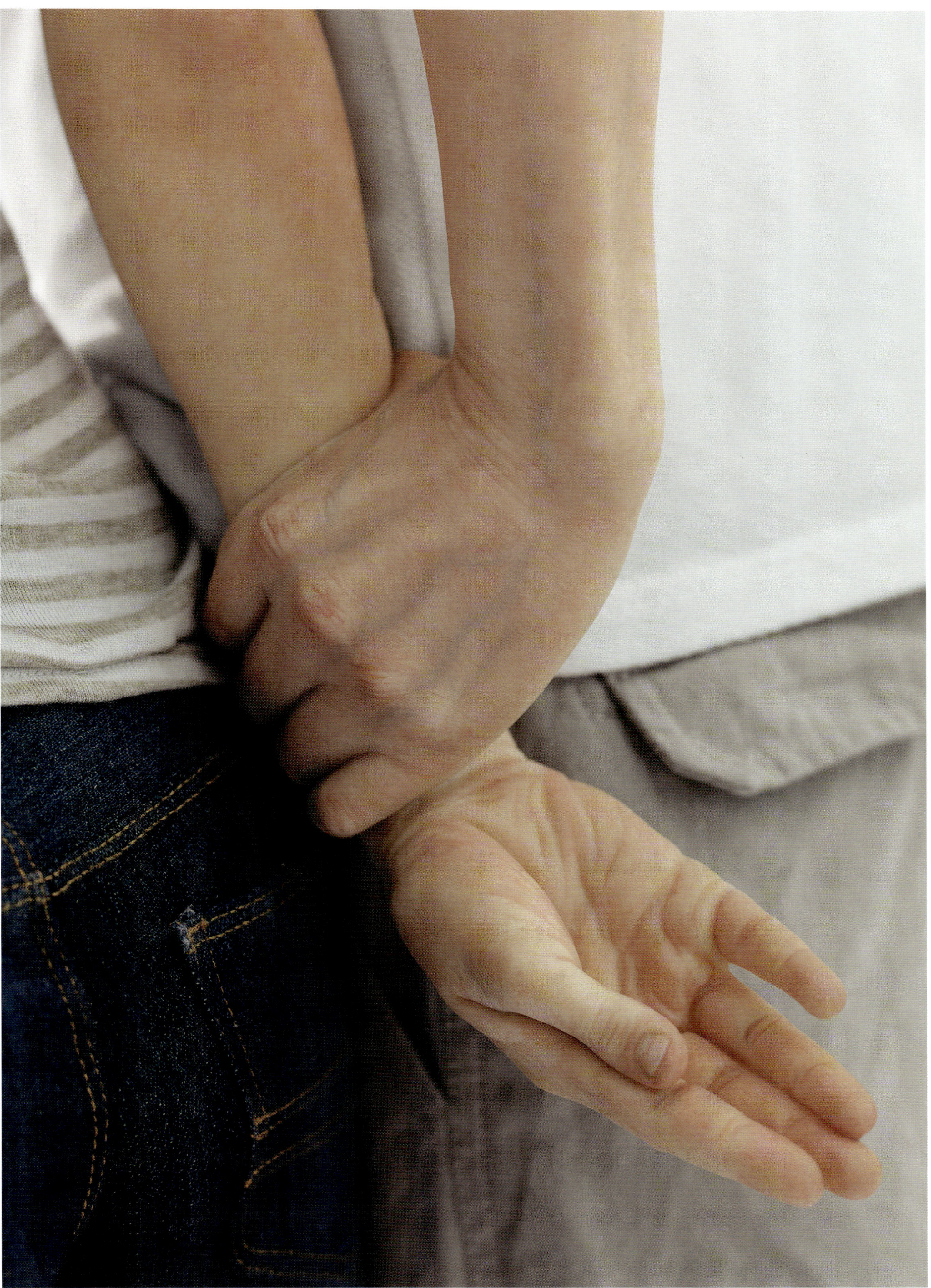

Dark Place 2018
140 × 90 × 75 cm

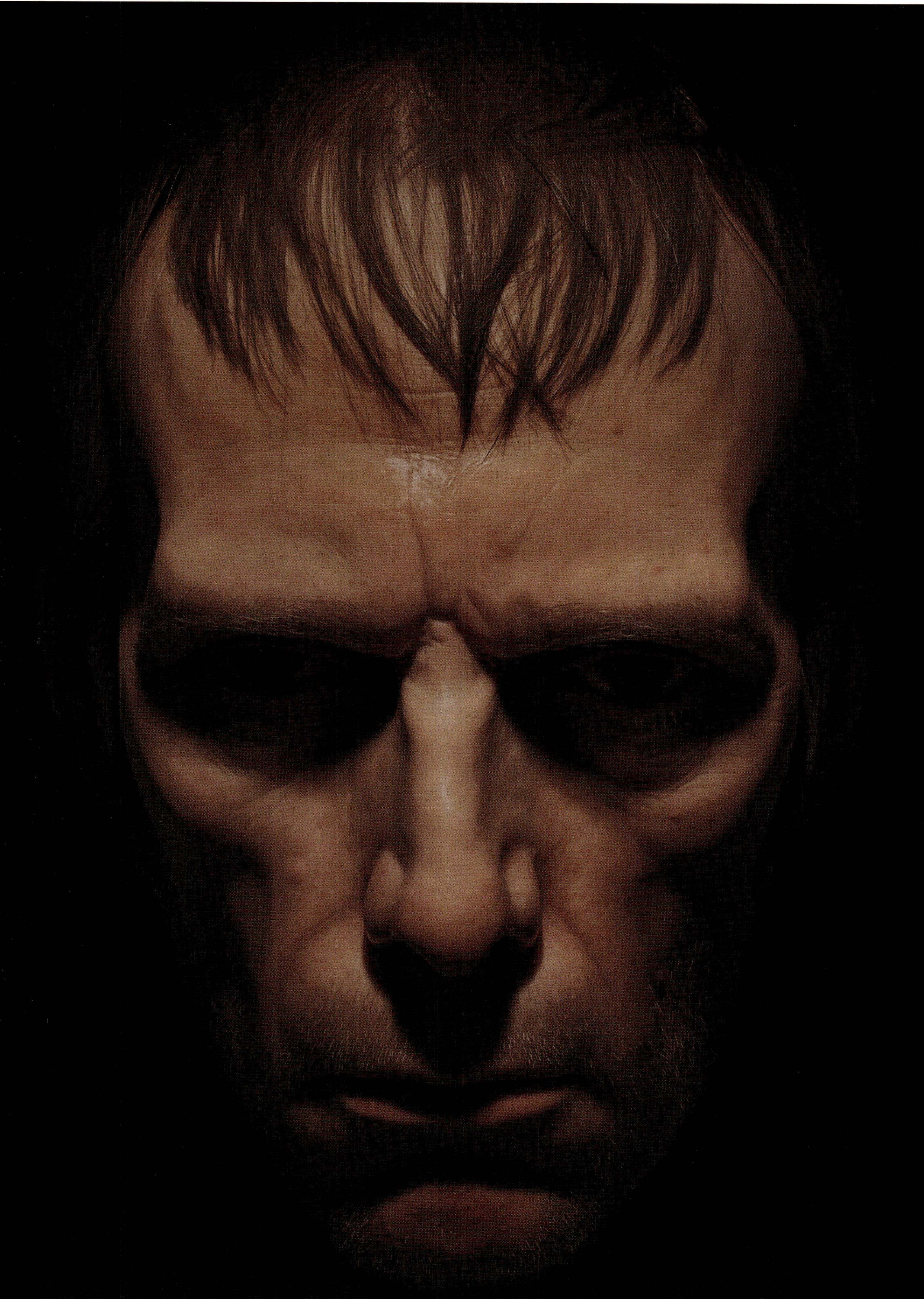

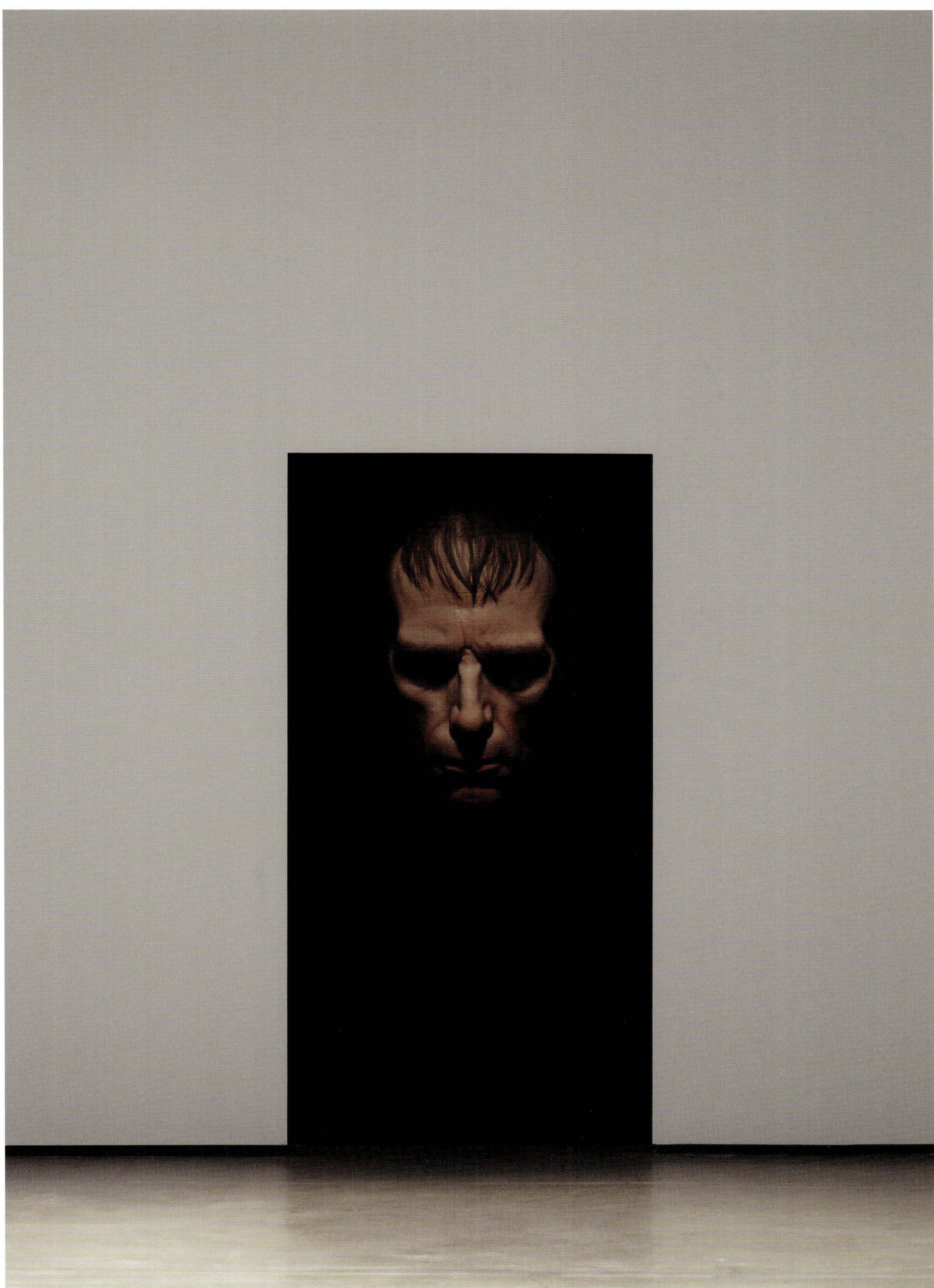

chicken/man 2019
80 x 140 x 86 cm

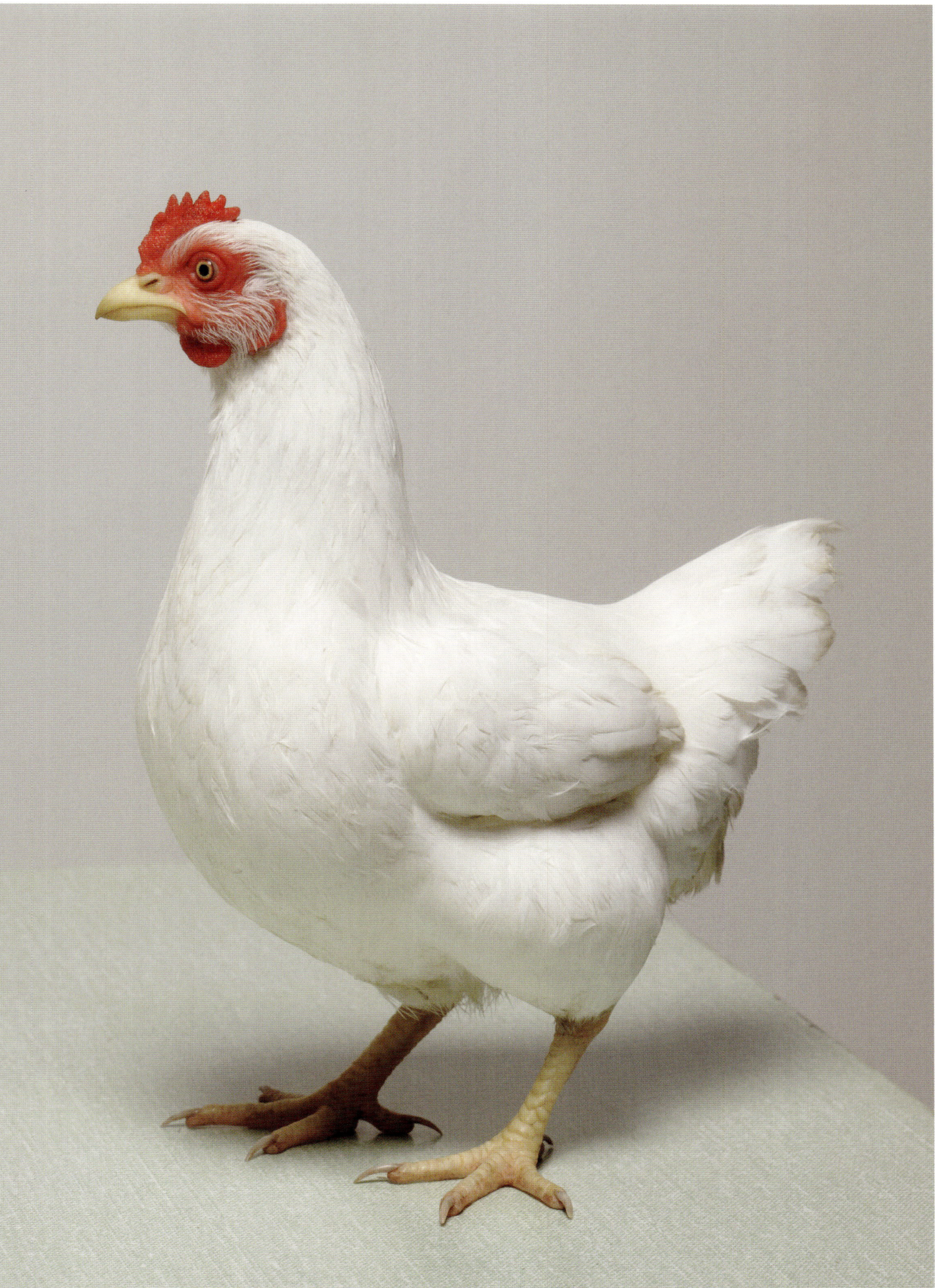

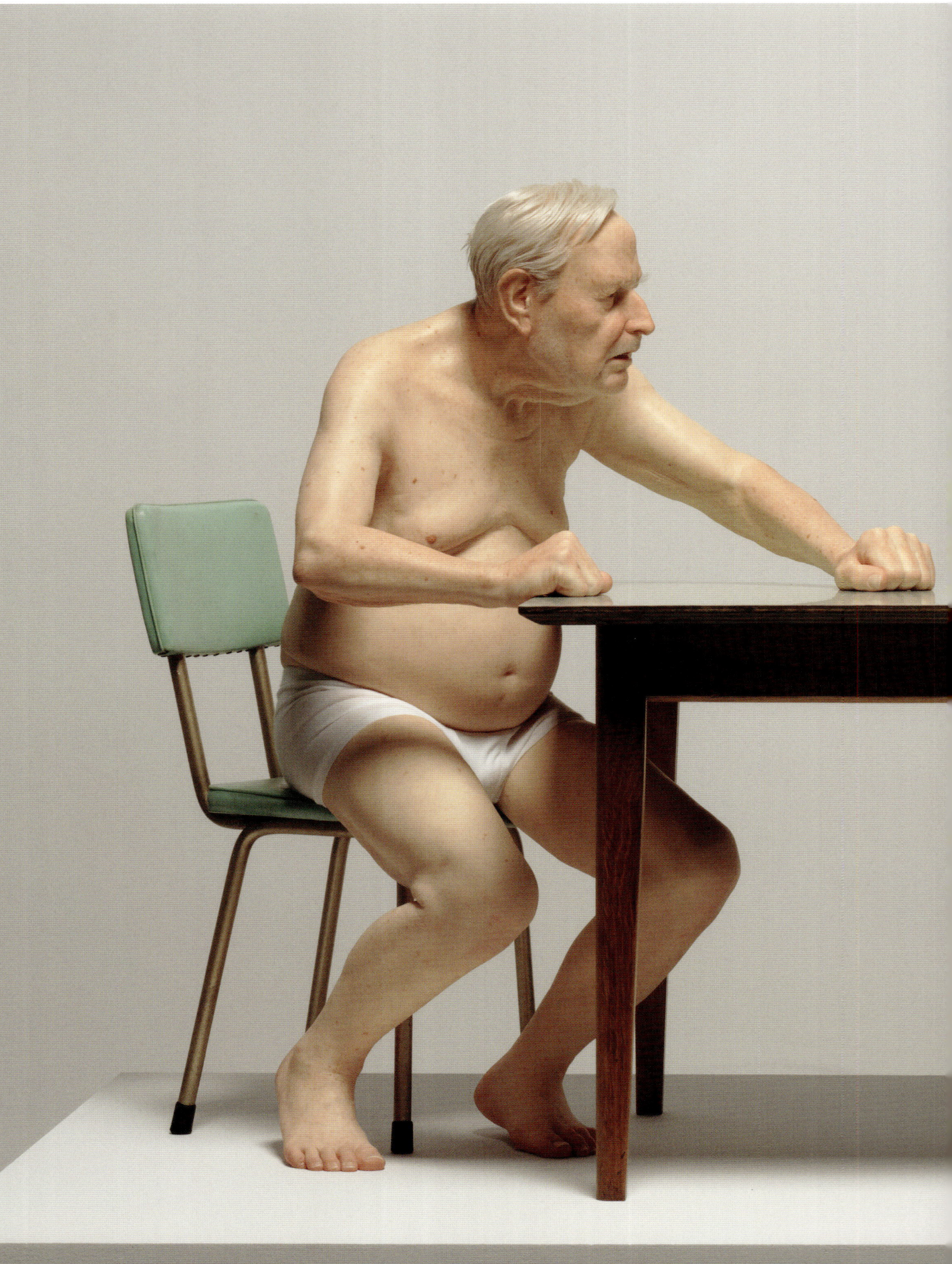

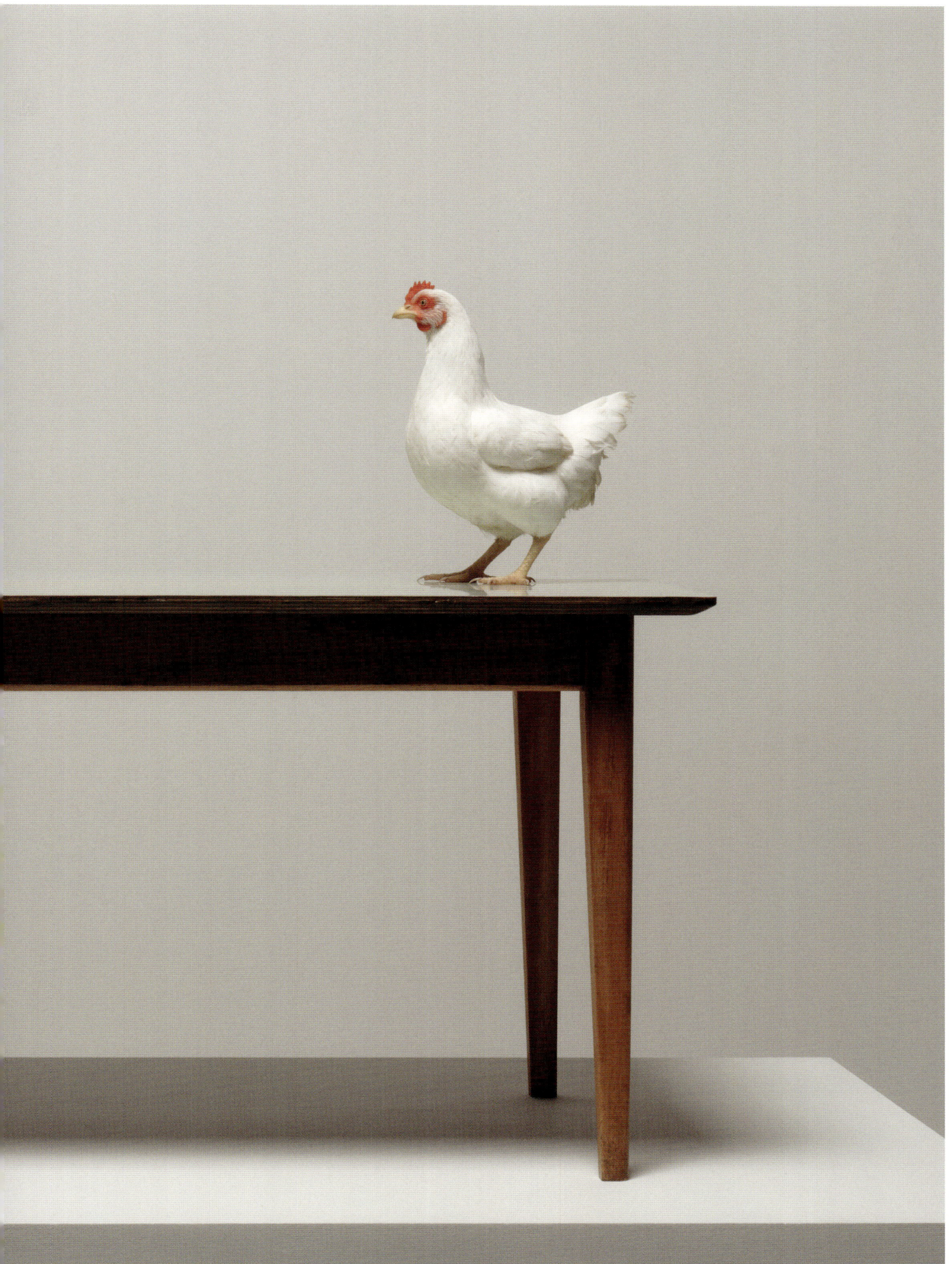

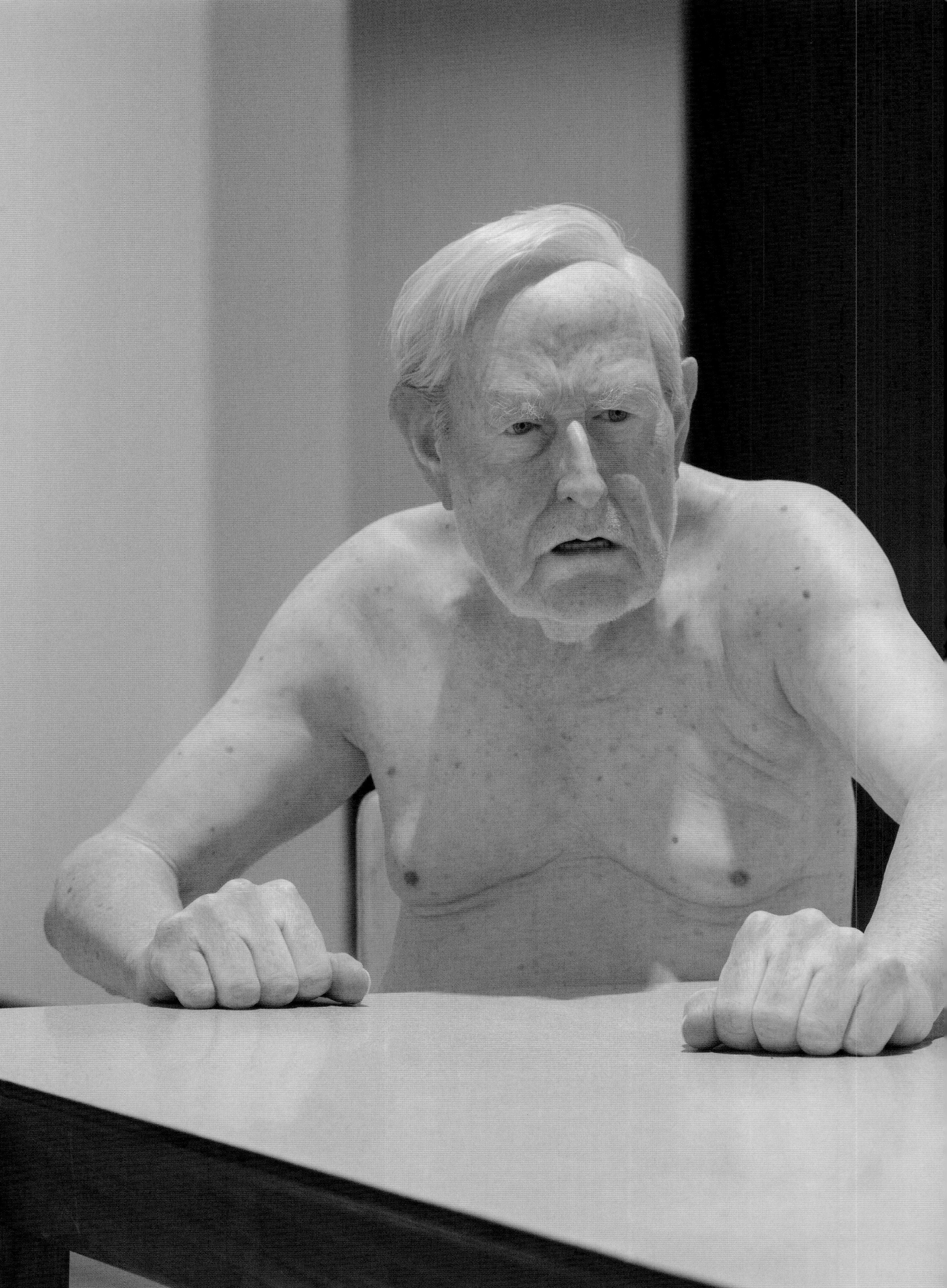

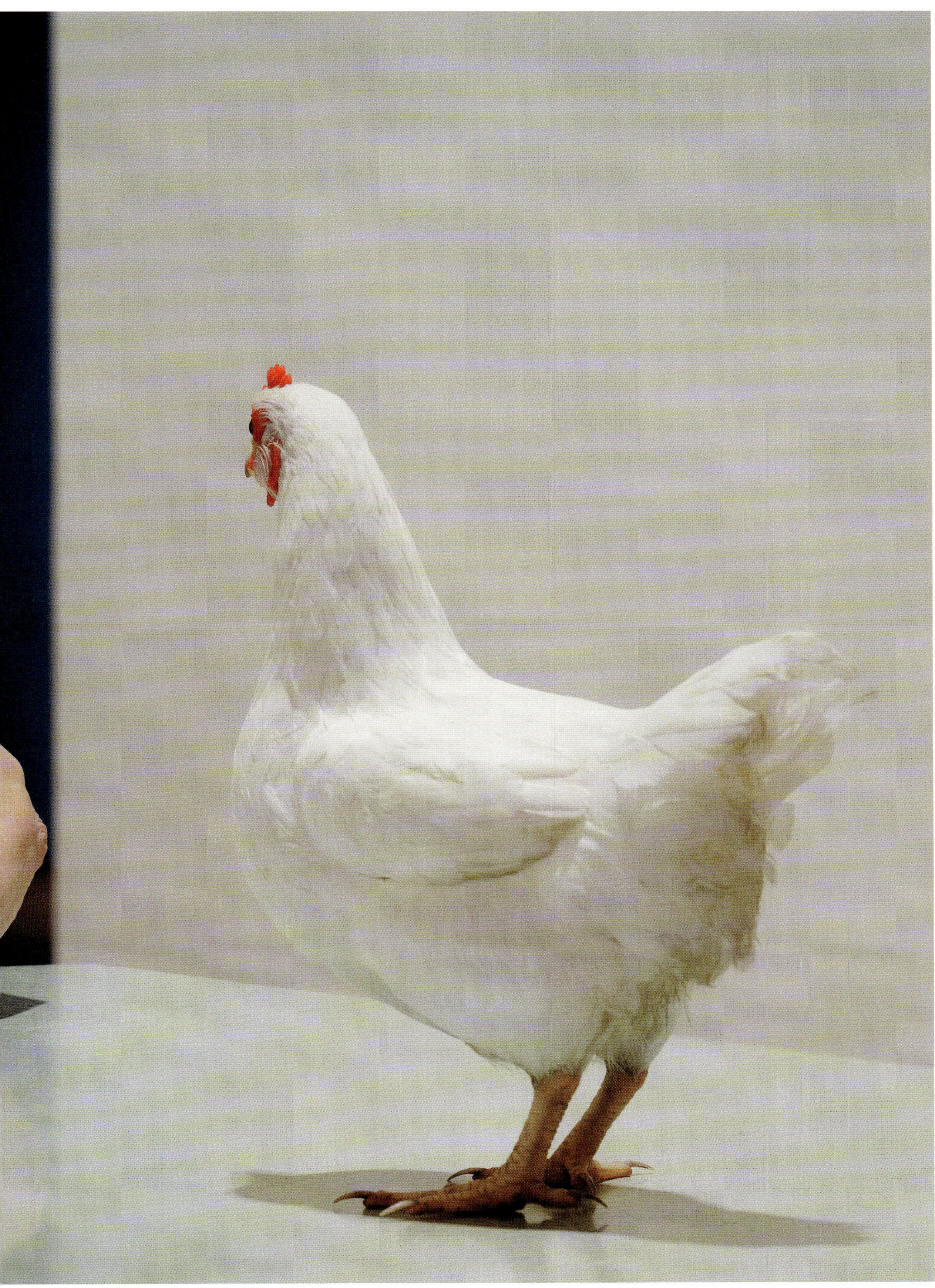

This Little Piggy 2023–25
(work in progress)
70 × 90 × 30 cm

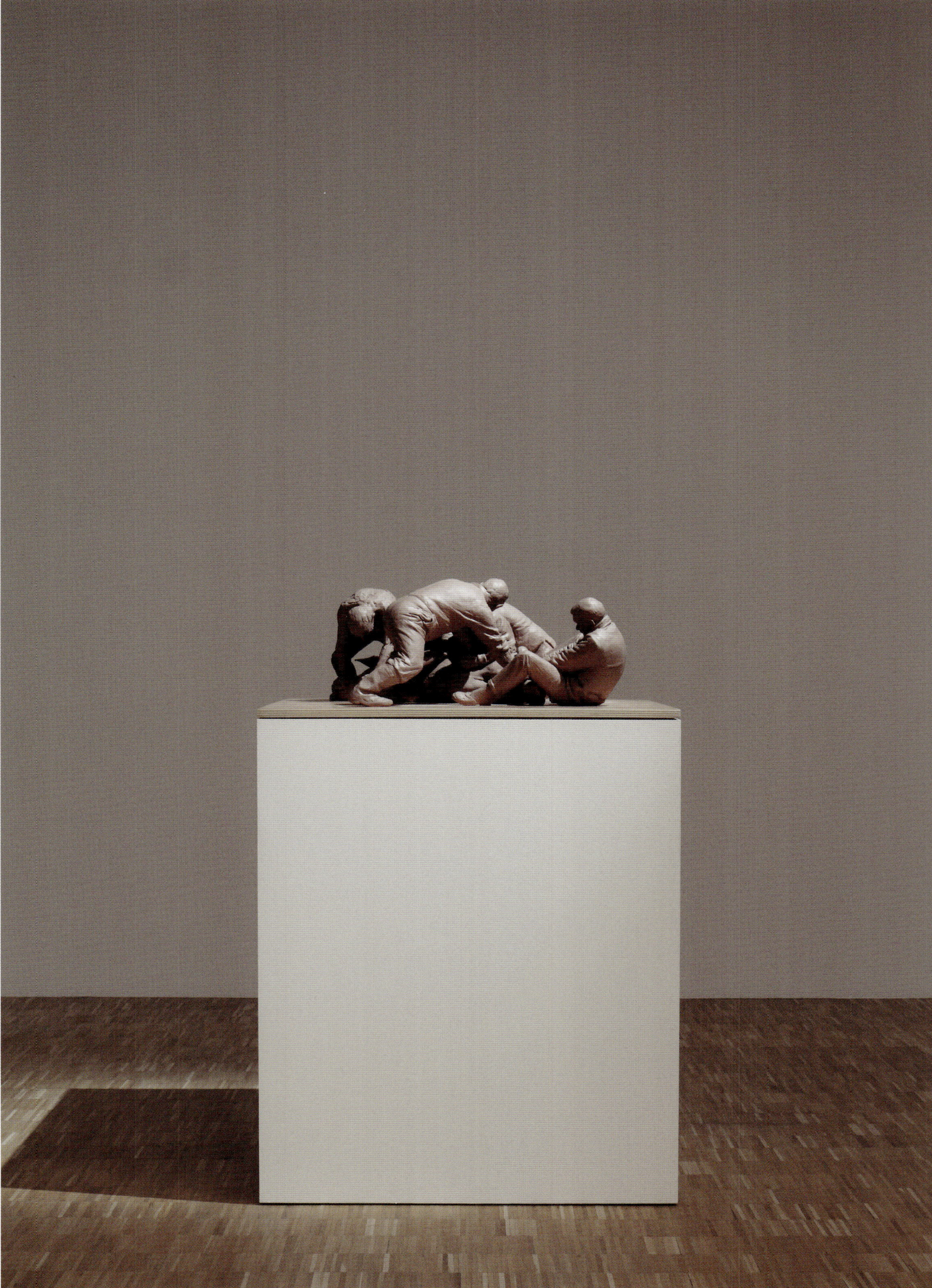

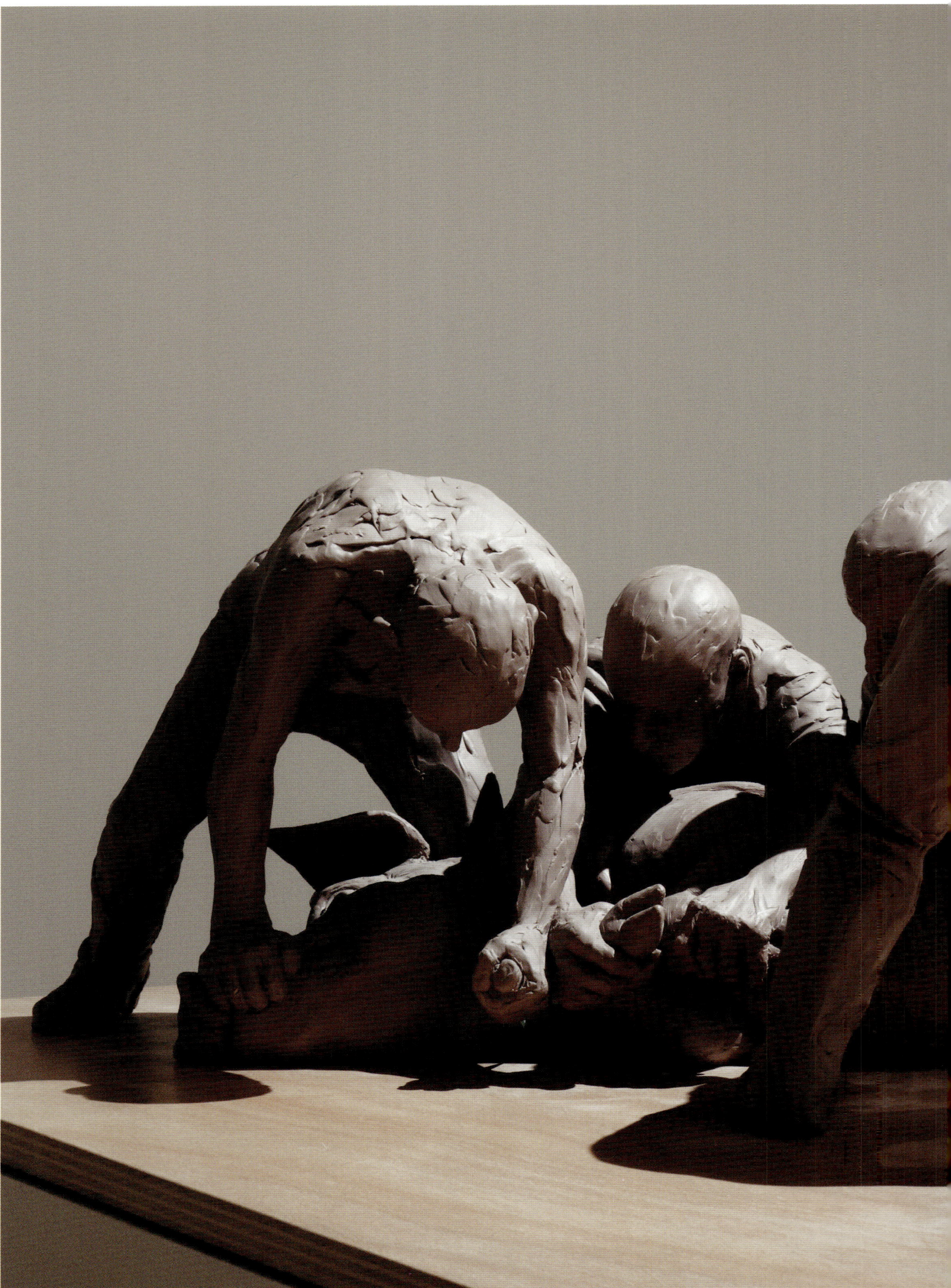

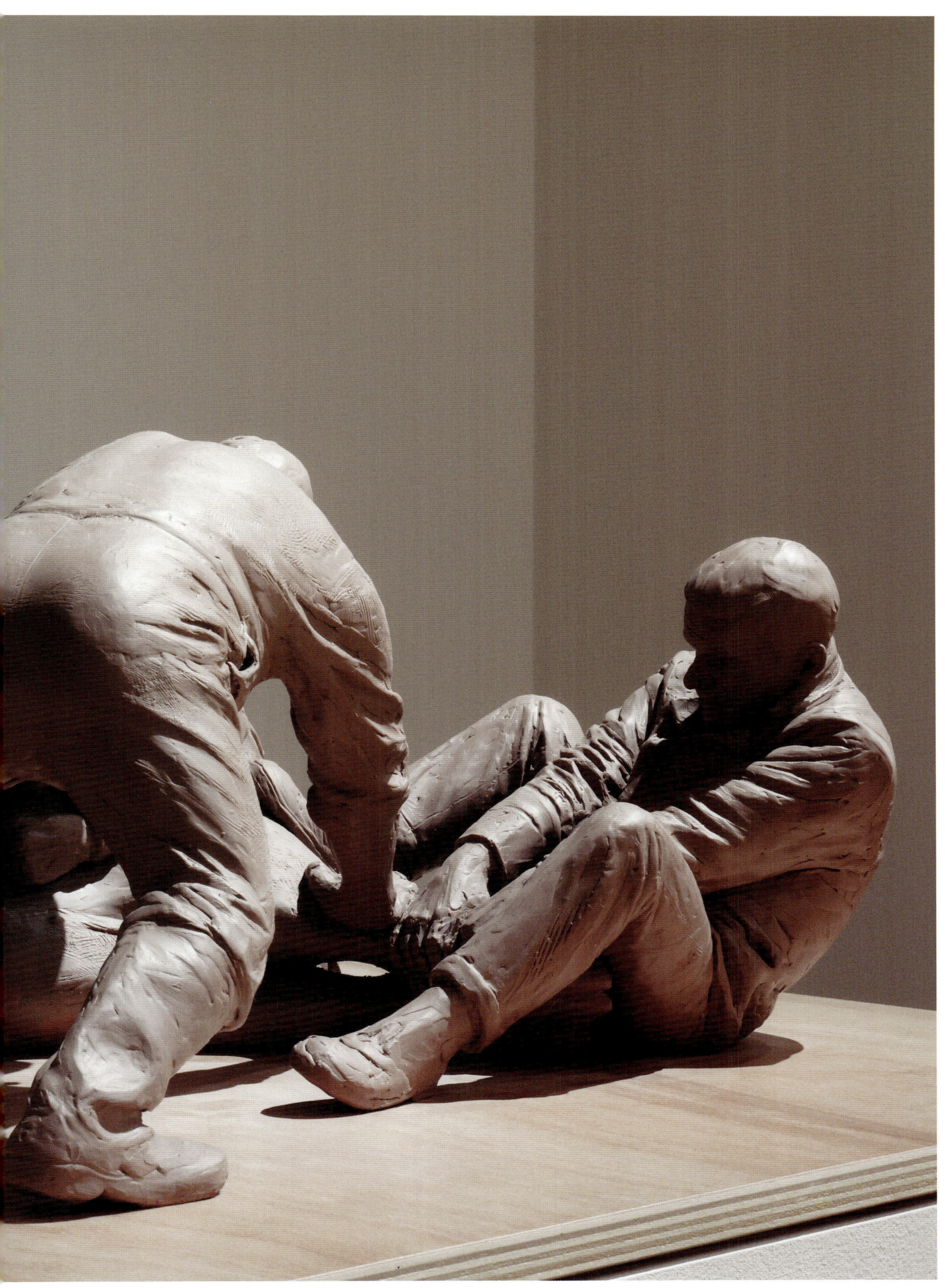

Havoc 2025
(work in progress)
dimensions variable

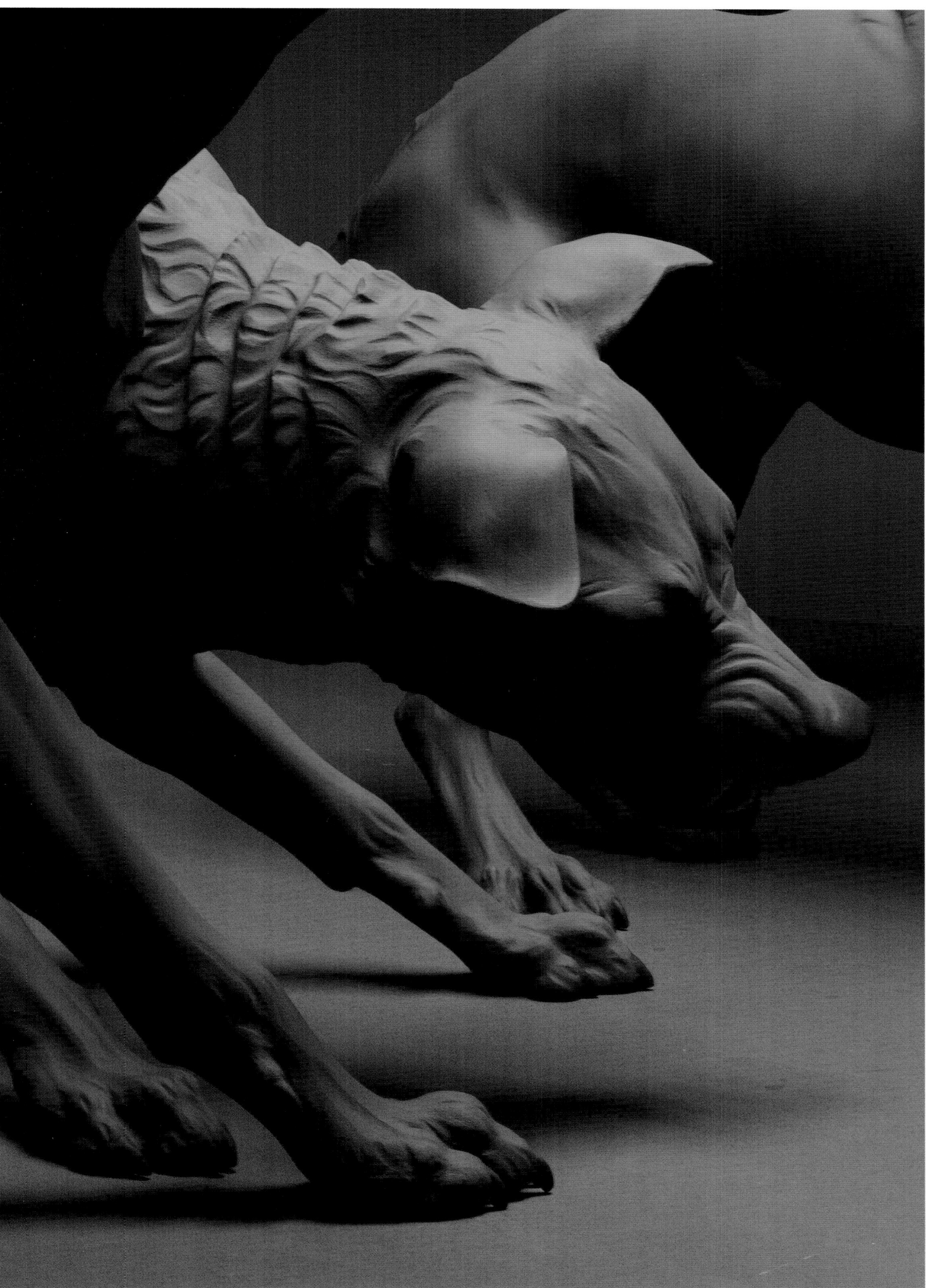

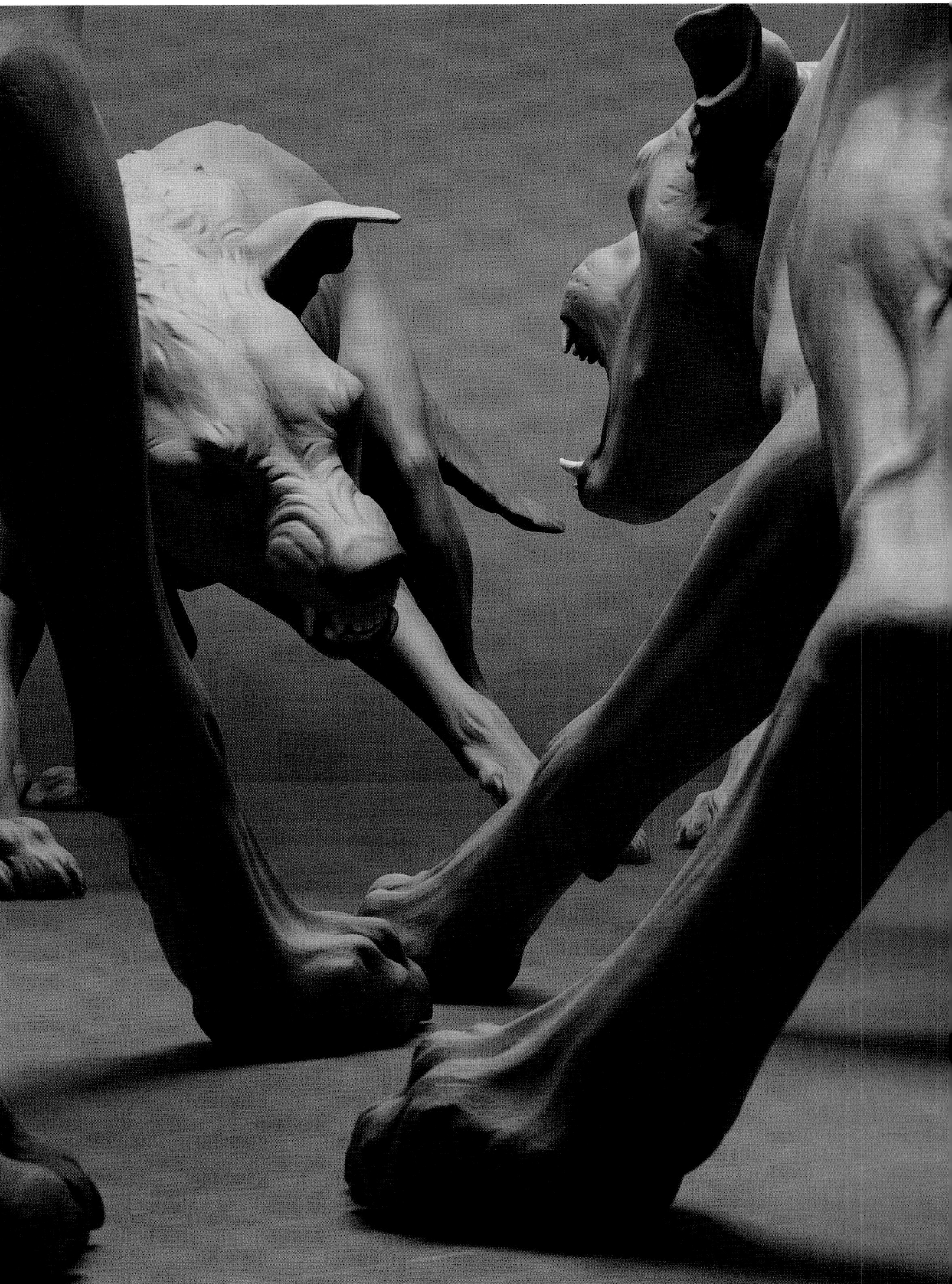

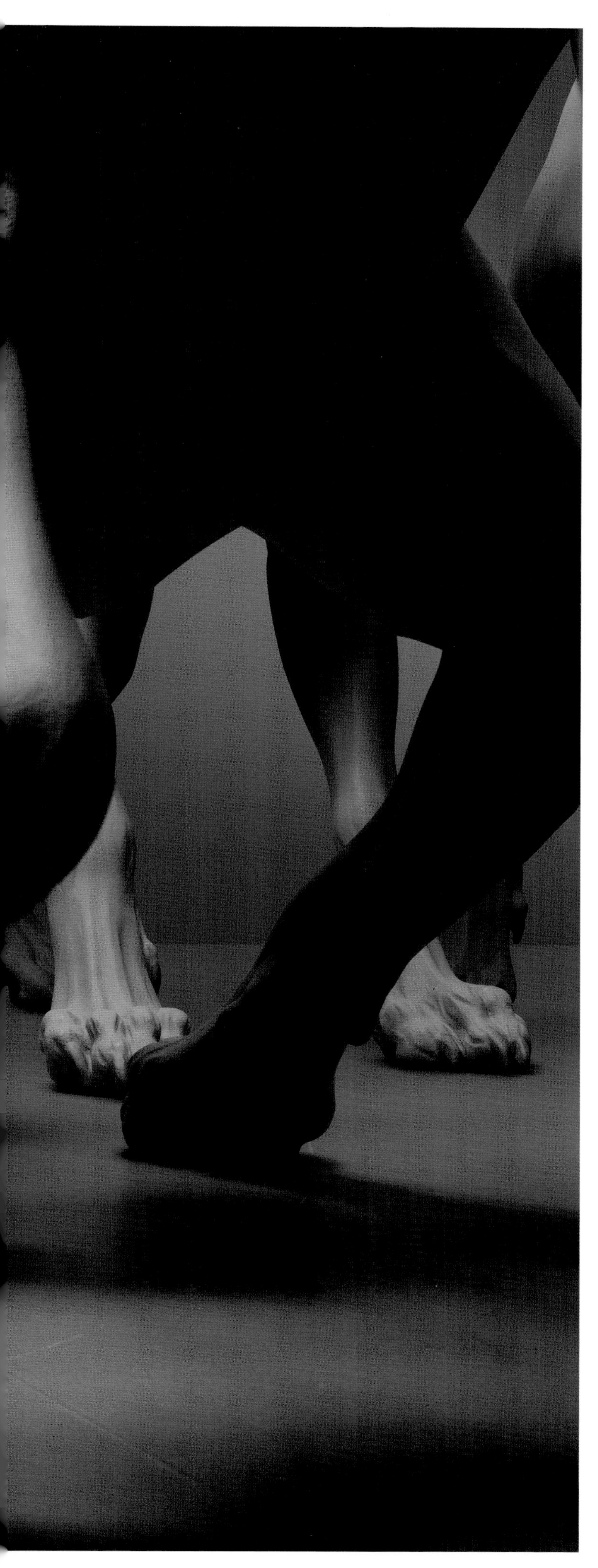

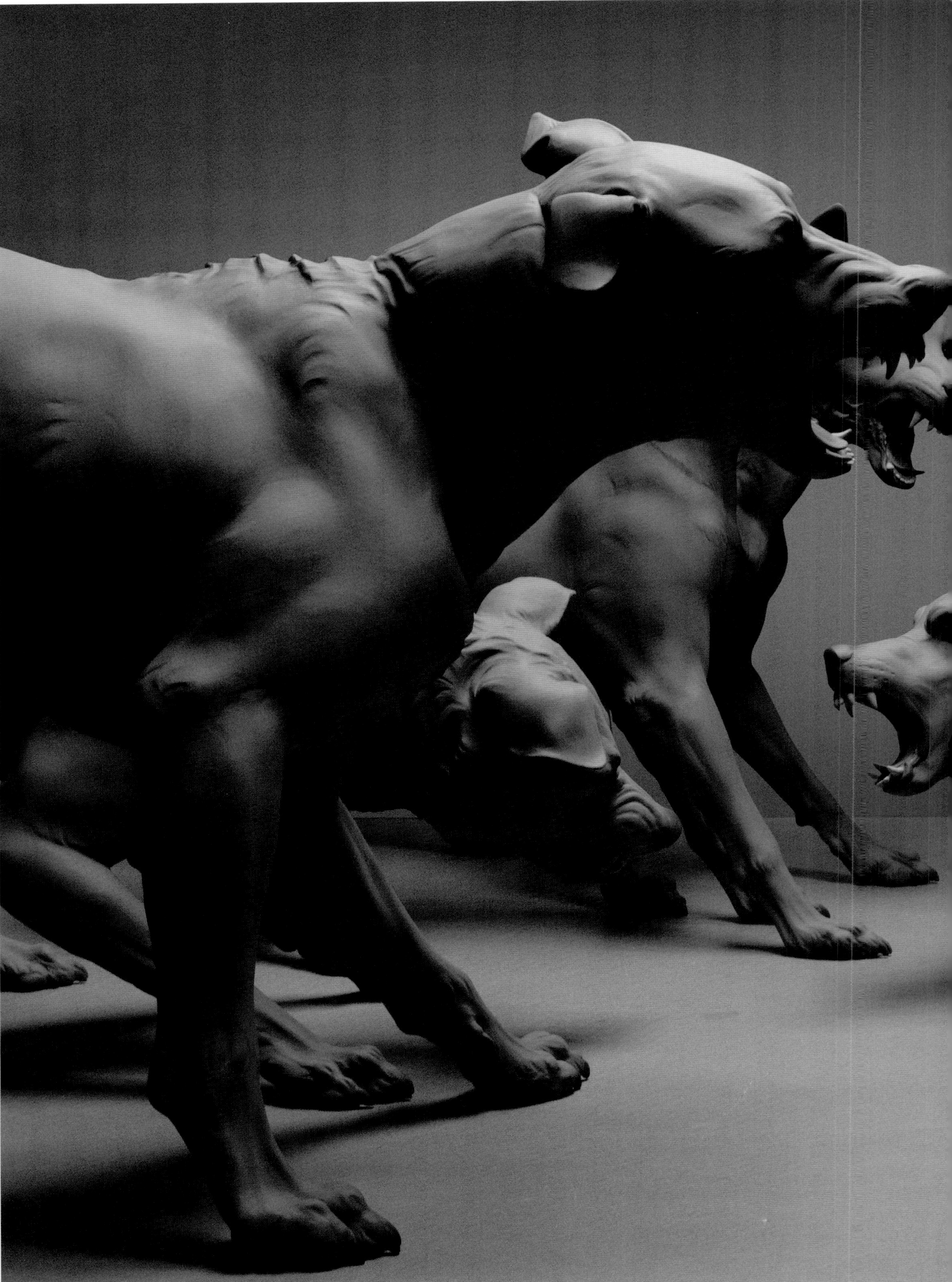

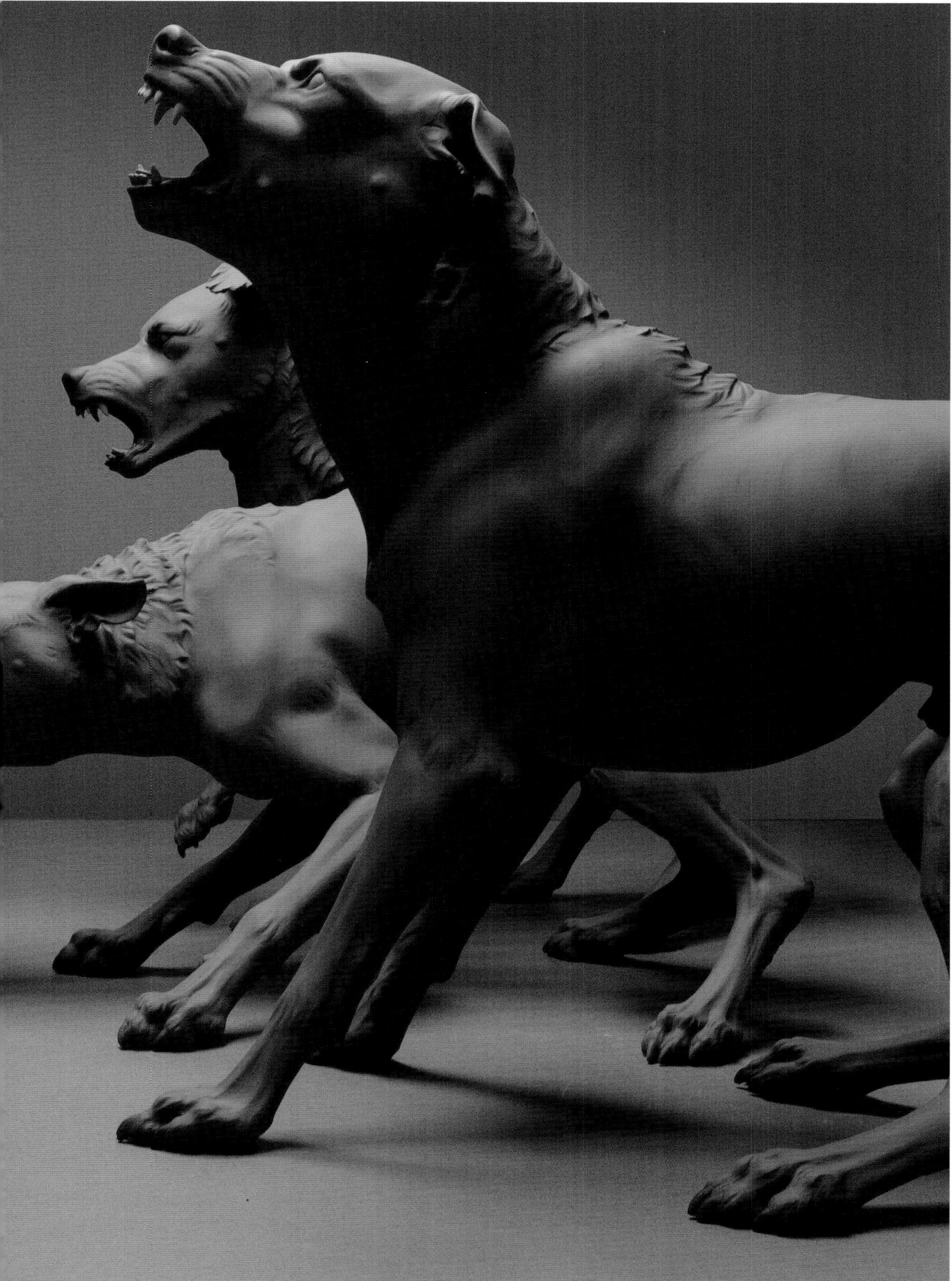

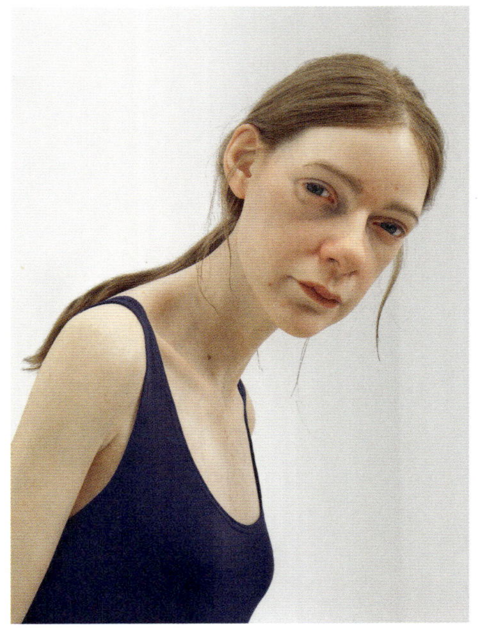

Ghost 1998/2014

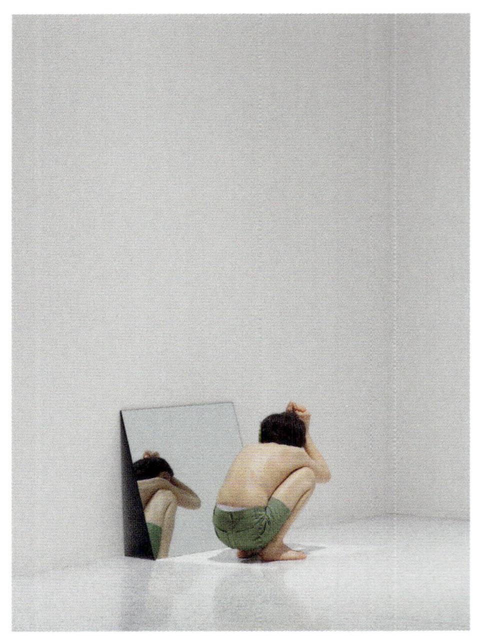

Crouching Boy in Mirror 1999–2002

Ron Mueck's *Ghost* is a vivid incarnation of adolescent self-consciousness. As though inhabiting her gawky growing body for the first time, testing how she takes up space, *Ghost* is a spirit shyly transitioning the states of child- and adulthood. The artist's almost unbearably tender insights into her feelings – not least her evident awareness of our presence – make it an exemplar of the artist's compassion, and potentially, ours.

But of course, this compassion is attached to a *sculpture*, not a human girl, and as such, Mueck the artist (as opposed to, say, Mueck the father – he has two daughters) must convey to us the personality, state of mind and situational awareness of his subject through purely sculptural means. It is through manifold artistic decisions – her stance, her lanky proportions, the expression of her 'body language' – that Mueck transmits *Ghost*'s inner world. The growth-spurt alien legs clutching the wall; the slight hunch and self-aware head turn, the cast of the eyes: all this Mueck inscribes in her body. As such, she – an inanimate object made of silicone rubber and fibreglass, finished with acrylic paint and lycra – invites the projection of our own embodied memories, sensory experiences, our very human feelings, to arrive at an empathic response that so closely mimics our human-to-human interactions.

Crouching Boy in Mirror emerged alongside its vastly larger twin, *Boy* 1999, one of Mueck's most famous pieces. At more than 4.5 metres tall, *Boy* is a monumental, rather quizzical character who first appeared in London's Millennium Dome in 2000, then squeezed into the Corderie at the Venice Biennale the following year before making his permanent home in the Danish city of Aarhus.

Crouching Boy in Mirror shares the quizzical nature of his gargantuan brother, but in its title, in the squatted pose of youthful flexibility, in its near exact size, it also recalls another famous sculpture: an enigmatic 'crouching boy' carved in marble by Michelangelo around 1530. What these boys share most is being caught, forever, in a moment of introspection.

Mueck's boy squats to look, maybe to withdraw; the mirror – long a symbol of self-knowledge, or deception – allows him to do both. The mirror's magic expands his space; once compact and tiny, it is now huge. While at first he looks to be alone, the mirror connects him, helping him establish his relationship with the world and secure his identity. From his crouch, he catches all who pass in an exchange of gazes – even those of his fellow fantastical Mueck beings.

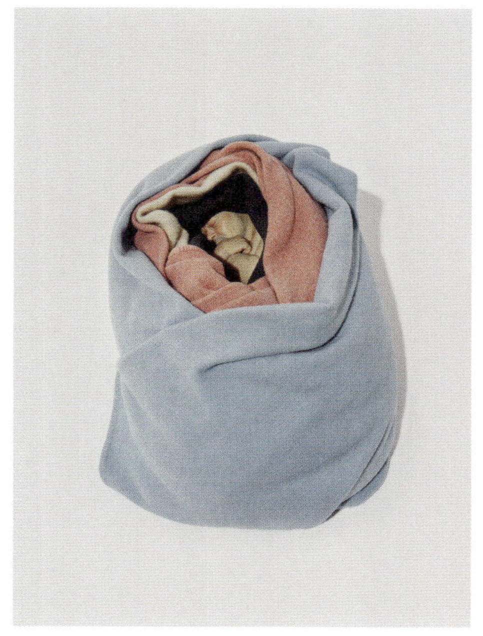

Man in Blankets 2000

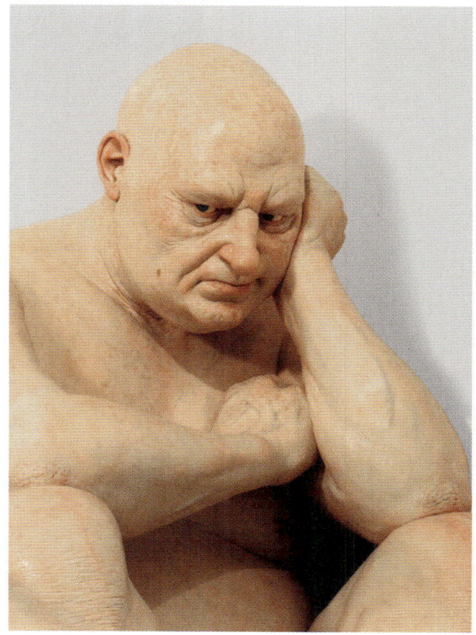

Big Man 2000

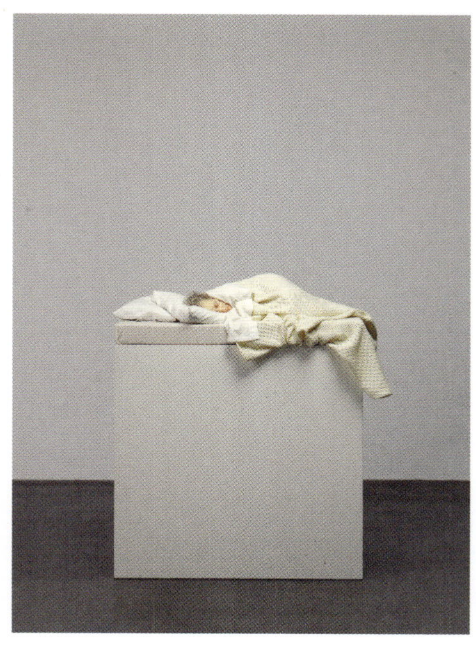

Old Woman in Bed 2000/2002

How tenderly can one feel towards an artwork? In *Man in Blankets*, Mueck affectionately cocoons his central figure in blankets, which offers some small protection at least. The whorled nest they form draws us down to the tiny man with distress (or annoyance) etched on his forehead. Is he deeply troubled, or does the bright light of the gallery, and our presence, simply irritate him and interrupt his determination to sleep?

The swaddled Lilliputian is preposterously part man, part infant (the 'bearded baby' as he is known at his home museum in the Netherlands). As such, though we see a man, we care about him – if we're so inclined – as we would a child. Mueck does not deceive us into caring, rather he produces an object about which we attach the concept of human care. The diminutive form of the *Man in Blankets* demarcates a staged space that recalls poet and literary critic Susan Stewart's insistence on 'the essential *theatricality* of all miniatures'.[1] Charity may be at the heart of this drama, but the script offers us no backstory. We can wonder if his situation is chosen or imposed, may worry at the institutional cast of his blankets, but there's a necessary and disquieting complexity to any answer. Sleeping, the man keeps his dreams secret.

Universally associated with gluttony, ribaldry and masculinity, the giant is a creature of surfeit and extravagance. Long yoked to the grotesque and the monstrous, the giant – especially a grumpy one – is a figure of our literary and cultural fantastic, from the heroes of Rabelais to Shrek.

Though *Big Man* seems a truly unruly giant fresh off the storybook page, he is in fact one of the few figures Mueck has modelled on a real live human. Mueck worked in the studio with a heavyset, naked and completely shaven model, after wanting to further explore the form of his miniscule, then recently completed, *Man in Blankets*. Frustrated at being unable to achieve the foetal pose Mueck sought, the model slumped down in the corner. Spied there by Mueck, a new scowling giant was born.

Scaled up in Mueck's hands, the *Big Man* becomes bigger, monumental, a feature of the landscape as much as a person (and, in the landscape of the gallery, he does what the gigantic always does, he transforms our body into a miniature). He may be big, but with his hairless body and his petulant side-eye, displaying an inability to emotionally regulate, he's perhaps less the 'monster among us' than a big baby.

Mueck's enhancement of emotional affect – both the outward expression of his subjects' interior states and our reaction to them – is the true focus of his art. *Old Woman in Bed*, inspired by a hospital visit Mueck made to a relative, is as affecting as they come.

The scale of this minute and frail figure magnifies her vulnerability, bringing her closer to the size of a baby at the opposite end of life. We feel her to be close to her last breath, believing, momentarily, that her unmoving shrouded silicone form seems entirely capable of respiration. Our hesitancy as to whether she is still (or was ever) breathing mirrors the experience of listening out for a loved one's ragged, possibly final, breath.

Just how is it that we can feel her to be close to death and, therefore, living? Mueck has withered her, isolated her on a plinth and engulfed her in institutional bed clothes. He has tinted her flesh the papery pallor of oxygen-starved skin, half-closed her unfocused eyes, and parted her lips to take in air. He has brought us to the limits of realism, but what we feel once we're there is dependent on our own experience, and the limits of our own compassion.

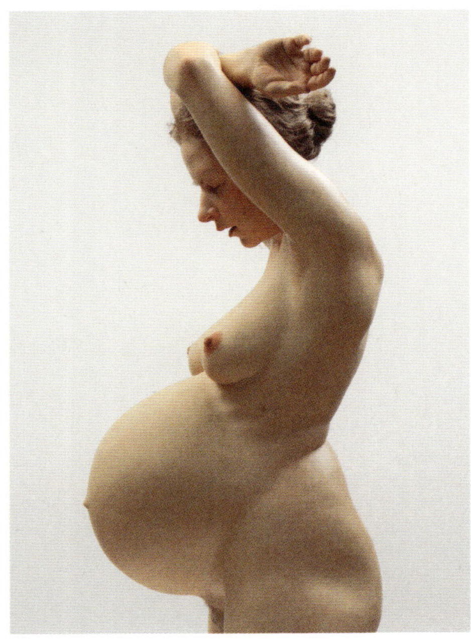

Pregnant Woman 2002

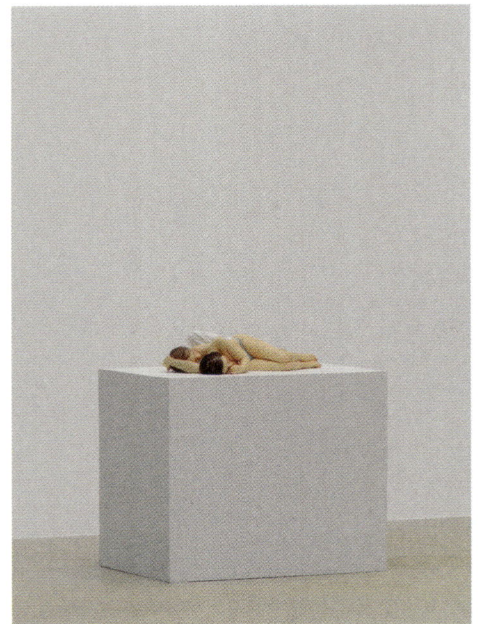

Spooning Couple 2005

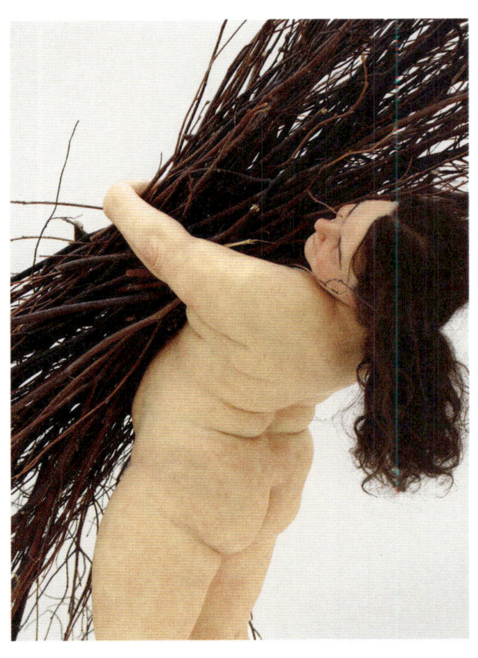

Woman with Sticks 2009–10

Pregnant Woman came into being while Mueck was resident artist at the National Gallery in London from 2000 to 2002. There, he encountered the many symbolic, often sacred, images of motherhood in the European art tradition – none of which tackled the subject of pregnancy, let alone its visceral physicality. For his image of motherhood, Mueck worked with a model over some months, right up till she gave birth just before the completion of the piece.

Mother and baby are about to experience the profound human moment that forms the original relationship: to be separated into two independent though tied entities through the life-changing encounter of birth. But Mueck's figure is not quite yet mother. Hugely outsized, it points less to her future role and focuses instead on the bodily impact of waiting and carrying. Exuding a weariness as overwhelming as its scale, it reveals evidence of a body near its limits for accommodating another – the dragging curve of the back, the central line of telltale hormonal fluctuation, the titanic bulge grounded through heavy legs. As tenderly as Mueck communicates this very *Pregnant Woman*'s condition, and her self-soothing strategies – turning inward, arms up making space, mouth open in a soft pant – her bodily sensations and the magnitude of the experience to come remain her own.

Spooning Couple is a work of sharp psychological tension. While the term 'spooning' implies the snug positioning of nestling bodies – like spoons in a drawer – any of its usual sense of affectionate familiarity is belied by the barely perceptible distance between these bodies. Spooning: the position's usual promise as a prelude or closure to sexual activity hints here at a failed or anxious physical encounter – though we will never know if the couple's apparent disposition betrays a passing reaction to a slight, an unrelated worry, or a relationship quietly unravelling.

Certainly, despite their intimacy, there's a distinct emotional distance cleaving this couple whose preoccupied facial expressions suggest not connectedness but estrangement. The body language of each figure reveals everything and nothing: *her*, legs stacked, core drawn up, hands pulled beneath her chin as a comfort; *him*, arm tight to his body, avoiding touch, though with one leg slipping forward (the only point of contact), betraying residual affection, even hope.

Mueck has made his *Spooning Couple* truly miniature, a scale that echoes the minute nuances of relationship dynamics. And, seen from above, this couple in its vulnerable state of half-dress draws us in to the intimacy of the scene, which has suddenly come to feel clinical, voyeuristic – crowded.

Woman with Sticks looks to have stepped right out of a fairytale. Not just any fairytale, one boldly reimagined for a post-feminist age by the likes of British writer Angela Carter, sensually and subversively centred on a strong female protagonist.

Yet, *Woman with Sticks* brings to mind the blurred boundaries of every fairytale or myth: the threshold zones between fiction and real life, human and non-human, animate and inanimate, familiar and strange. And like any proper enchanted lead character, she appears to have been charged with an epic quest, an impossible labour. We imagine her undisclosed task (her burden of sticks) to be as mindless and endlessly repeated as the nightly weaving and unpicking undertaken by Penelope awaiting the return of Odysseus in Homer's ancient Greek epic.

She's an unsettling archetype, Mueck's strong and improbably naked woman, the embodiment of Sigmund Freud's 'uncanny': something familiar that has been made strange only through repression.[2] She exhibits the traces of her labours in her bowed posture and the fine (perfectly proportioned) scratches on her skin. Her disarming (if miniaturised) realism matches a disarmingly direct gaze that crosses into the land of the living. She turns on us a glinting, knowing eye that dares us to cross the threshold and join her.

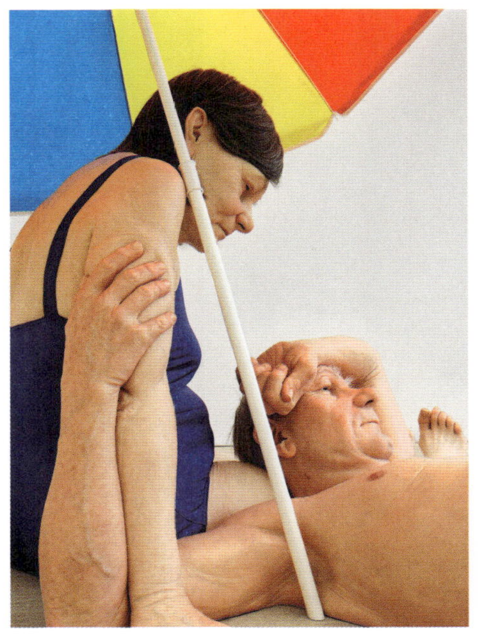

Couple Under an Umbrella 2013

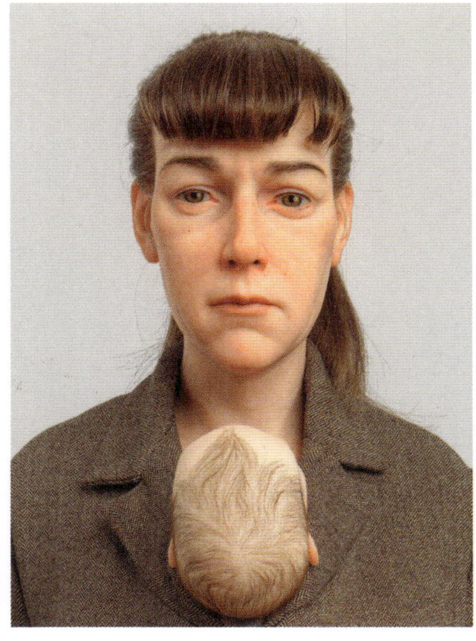

Woman with Shopping 2013

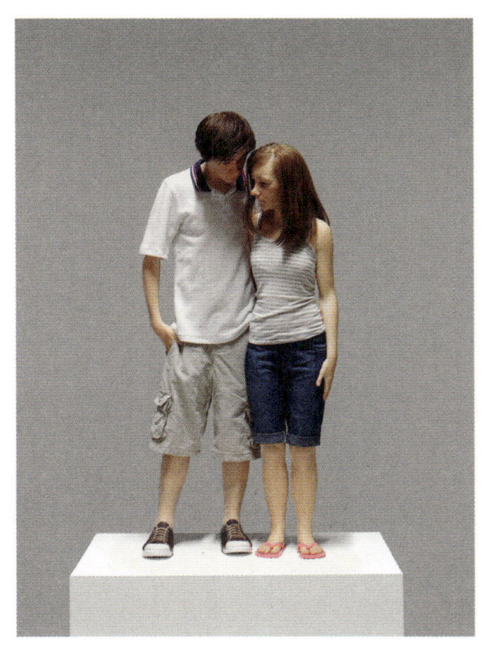

Young Couple 2013

While many of Mueck's cast of characters are literally and emblematically solitary, many form pairs that sharply focus attention on the very subject of 'relationship'. Whether a mother and infant child, a young dating couple, or a man and a chicken, Mueck's pairs see him expand beyond singular traits and predicaments to probe the ambiguous tensions of partnership.

We encounter *Couple Under an Umbrella* in a moment of stillness; a scene suggestive of the beach where bodies are usually both relaxed and at their most exposed. Here, under the harsh light not of the sun but of the gallery, Mueck places his couple under the protection of a unifying umbrella. The discrete vignette it creates freezes in space and time what we might assume to be the many years of their long union.

If the meticulous detailing is precise – the grip of toes, pressure of fingers on skin, a wedding ring long embedded in flesh – the sentiment of their connection, though intimate, is inscrutable. Are their separated and cryptic gazes affectionate, bored or plain bitter? Is their practised pose reciprocally supportive, or one-sided and uncomfortable? Mueck might be guiding us to reflect on the apparent constancy of their relationship, or he just might be pointing out its potential for enmity and malignancy.

While Mueck's sculptures get us thinking about big themes like birth and death, love and fear, his compassionate vignettes often document apparently inconsequential everyday interactions. Mueck's *Woman with Shopping* – a sleep-deprived young woman and baby whom he passed briefly on a London street (and sketched on the only paper to hand, an old parking ticket) – is no less wrenching for his having shunned the momentous for the fleeting and negligible.

Woman with Shopping is one of Mueck's many works featuring mothers and babies, both together and separate. Here, the pair appears detached, their two estranged selves producing a piteous image of alienation. Does Mueck suggest the profound existential crises of mothers and the micro-traumas of infancy, or something more mundane? Is she post-partum depressed? Enduringly, or merely momentarily, weary? Lonely, unappreciated or simply bored ... all options seem entirely fitting for a young mother carrying the load. And what of baby, who tries so hard to connect? Neglected, dejected, alert or just hungry (again), the baby remains unseen or ignored within the undisclosed yet compelling narrative.

Mueck presents his diminutive teen sweethearts just as he encountered them – on the street: one of the quiet, unremarkable moments he's drawn to. At first glance, *Young Couple* reveals itself to be a study of youthful affection. With Mueck, though, glancing is never enough; it pays to stare.

The pair appears to be close, if somewhat disconnected. Mueck maps with precision their ordinary and intimate details – the mirroring of their casual dress, heads tilted together (but down, obliquely, away from us and apart from each other). Then, moving around them, we see that grip: the girl's wrist so tightly, too tightly, held. That gesture (and that of her own suddenly stiffened left hand) changes everything. What is it that we see? A desperate reassurance, a misplaced attempt at protection, the red flag of possessive coercion? However we come to read it, one ambiguous gesture has punctured our image of innocence, turning a sweet moment sour. During our encounter with the work, our perspective has shifted and with it its 'truth' – which of course, Mueck reminds us, can never be known. Are they even lovers, or a bullying brother and stubborn sister? Mueck's snapshot makes the verdict uncertain. All we can trust – or doubt – is our instinct.

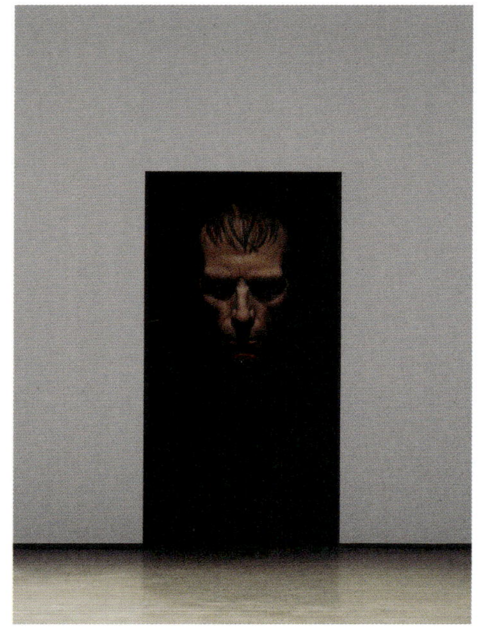

Dark Place 2018

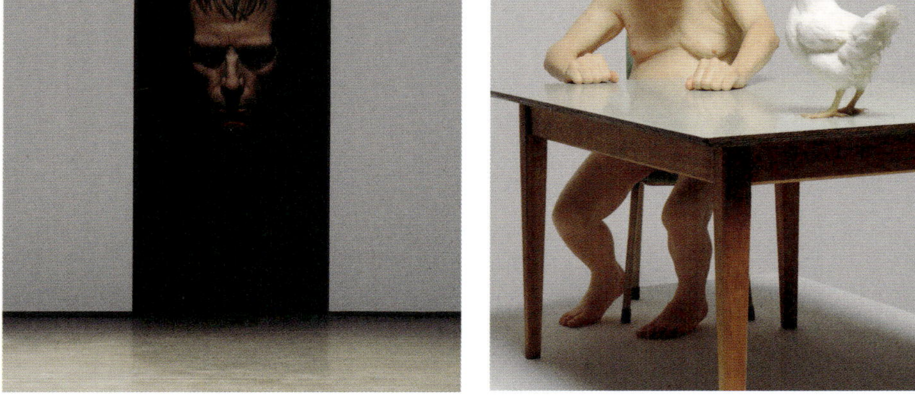

chicken/man 2019

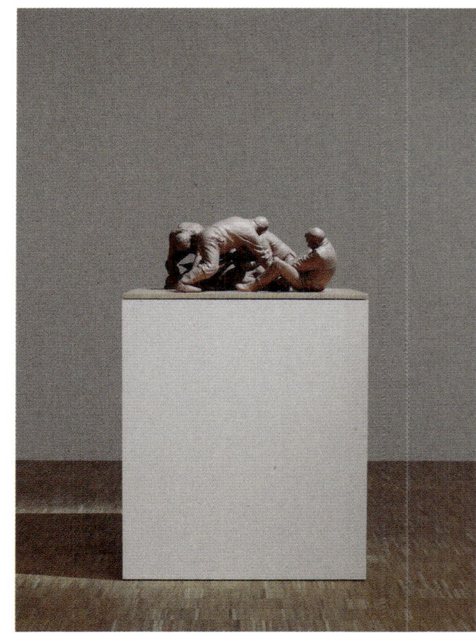

This Little Piggy 2023–25

In *Dark Place*, Mueck puts some distance between us and his looming melancholy subject, a troubled, dark-thinking friend. An intense portrait, formally it follows directly from *Mask I*, *II* and *III*, three giant works Mueck created between 1997 and 2005. Like them, it functions – at least in part – by heightening our awareness of the space our bodies occupy. *Dark Place* also shares with several of Mueck's newer works a subtle recasting of our relationship with the architectural space of the art museum – something that continues in the newest work, *Havoc*.

Mueck creates in *Dark Place* a gloom both literal and figurative, folding form and content into an uncustomarily theatrical space that is limiting, claustrophobic, affective. It is one of Mueck's most overtly gothic works. The gothic, that aesthetic of darkly romantic terror and mysterious haunting, has often appeared in the margins of Mueck's practice; here, it introduces an existential threat that also poses a challenge to the limits of empathy and compassion. As viewers left on a darkened threshold, we may feel sympathy or fear, but we are unable to inhabit the same space, we can't enter its shadows. Is this, perhaps, as close as we get to understanding the pain of another? Are the emotions we ultimately confront on that threshold our own?

For all its absurdity, *chicken/man* is one of the most rooted in the 'real' of all Mueck's works. It is a portrayal of an old family friend from the Isle of Wight in England, where Mueck has his studio, and an unidentified chicken – as much lovingly, exactingly wrought portrait as curiously incongruous scenario.

The space between our protagonists is so charged that it drives us to seek a non-existent backstory. Facing off as they do, these two radiate an intense emotional bond. Are they opponents, friends, figments of the imagination? The man: all puzzlement, spotted and softened by age, flesh sagging, personality almost known. The chicken: watchful, fashioned from dove feathers to the scale of the half-sized man. Framing them, the strictly scaled and patinaed table and chair that have become characters with their own, albeit imagined, history.

Seeking a fitting partner for his friend, Mueck immediately knew he had 'just the right blend of the mundane and the surreal' when a chicken came to mind.[3] Their pairing forms a compelling dialogue about unknowability – of the situation in which they find themselves, of our fellow creatures, of the ultimate opaqueness of a work of art.

A compelling study of active bodies in space, *This Little Piggy* advances Mueck's move away from perfect surface fidelity towards a naked concentration of form, gesture and active pose. This is the first showing of the traditionally modelled group as a finished piece, having been previously exhibited in clay as a work in progress.

The 'group' is still rare in Mueck's oeuvre, which for many years favoured solitary figures and only more recently couples. Here, both human and animal figures form a concise tableau, a vivid, living scene whose dynamic choreography draws us in. For all that life, the group is in a death struggle, either working as one on the difficult task of slaughter or strenuously engaged, alone, in the matter of survival.

Evoking the dark side of the nursery rhyme that begins 'This little piggy went to market', Mueck's creation takes us to the realm of fairytale, something passed down as both primal and familiar. The scene was inspired by *Pig Earth*, John Berger's stories of brutal traditional life in rural France. Like Berger, Mueck works with a graphic economy to inhabit a place between fiction and documentary, a sort of violent fable set within the real violence of everyday life.

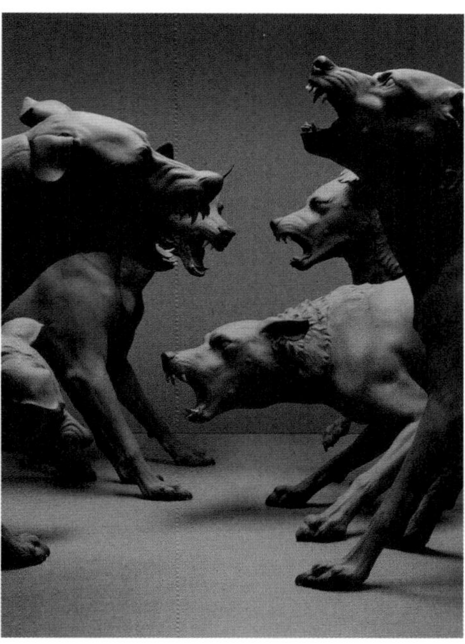

Havoc 2025

The dogs in Mueck's *Havoc* are the stuff of nightmares, conjured from some ancient mythic source, from memory itself. Big enough and mean enough to do some damage, we can tell ourselves all we want that they were born in clay and finished in resin, but we surely hesitate before stepping in among them.

Mueck has been working away at the subject of dogs for years. Three of them emerged in 2023 as the sculpture *En Garde*: huge, black and forbidding, but stilled and enigmatic. *Havoc* brings things to a head, two fierce packs choreographed at the very moment of attack. They fully express Mueck's recent evolution from mimetic surface realism towards essential form and manifest action. Energetic, emotional, theatrical yet entirely lifelike, in their muscular distillation and baroqueness they recall the sculptures of Bernini (most especially his Cerberus, the multi-headed guard dog of the underworld and the writhing bodies it patrols, in *Rape of Proserpina* 1621–22).

With their menacing scale, snarling maws and raised hackles, the dogs bring Mueck's customary anxious uncertainty – not just ours, *theirs* – to a crescendo. Already made tense by our troubled times, we walk among them and become embroiled in the fight. Mueck summons the hounds of hell as a warning to us all: this is dangerous.

1 Susan Stewart, *On longing: narratives of the miniature, the gigantic, the souvenir, the collection*, Duke University Press, Durham/London, 1993, p 54.
2 Sigmund Freud, 'The "Uncanny"' (1919) in *The standard edition of the complete psychological works of Sigmund Freud*, trans James Strachey, vol xvii, Hogarth Press, London, 1955, p 241.
3 Mueck, quoted in Lara Strongman, 'Studio visit, Ron Mueck', *Bulletin*, B.196, 29 May 2019, christchurchart gallery.org.nz/bulletin/196/studio-visit, accessed 15 Jun 2025.

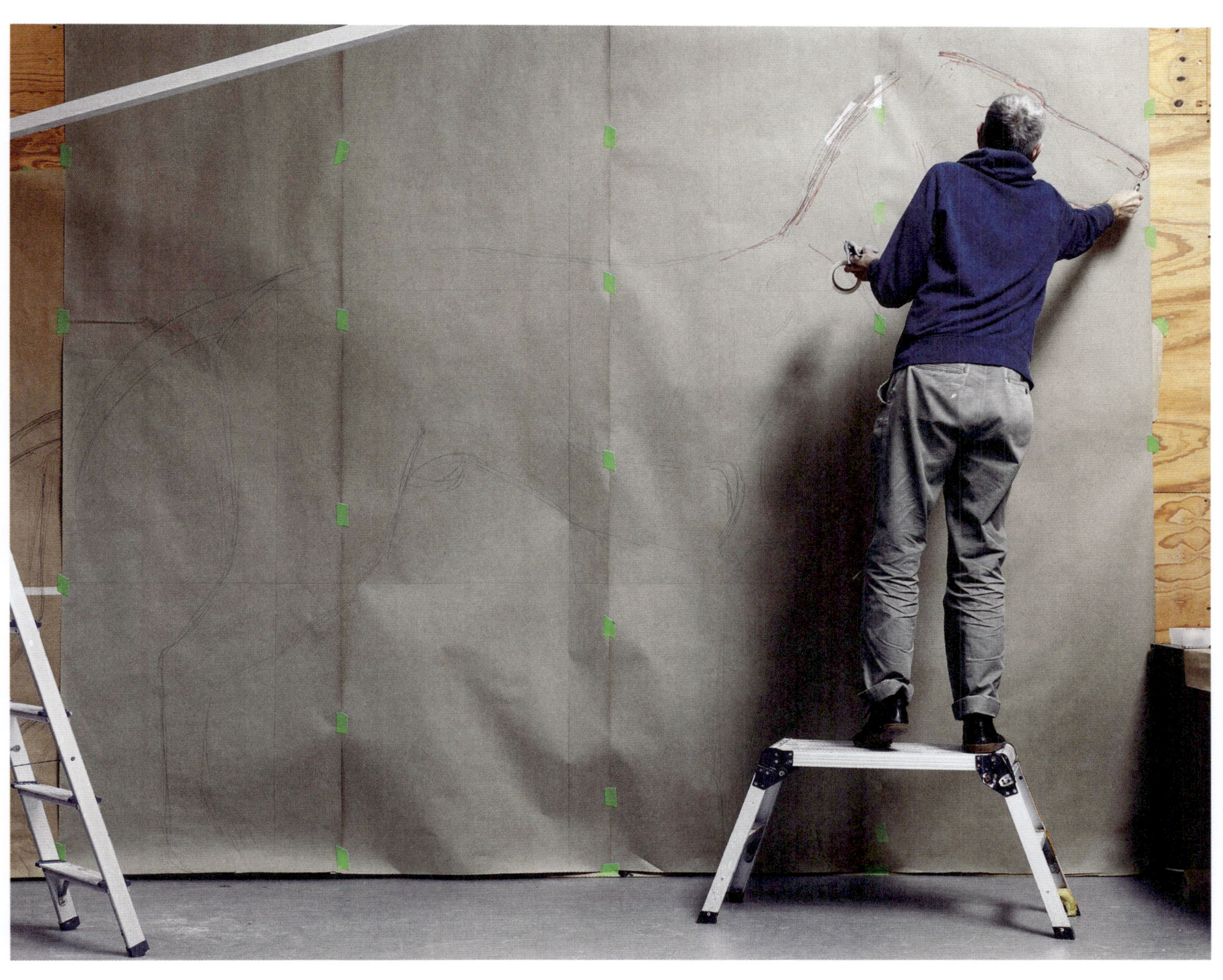

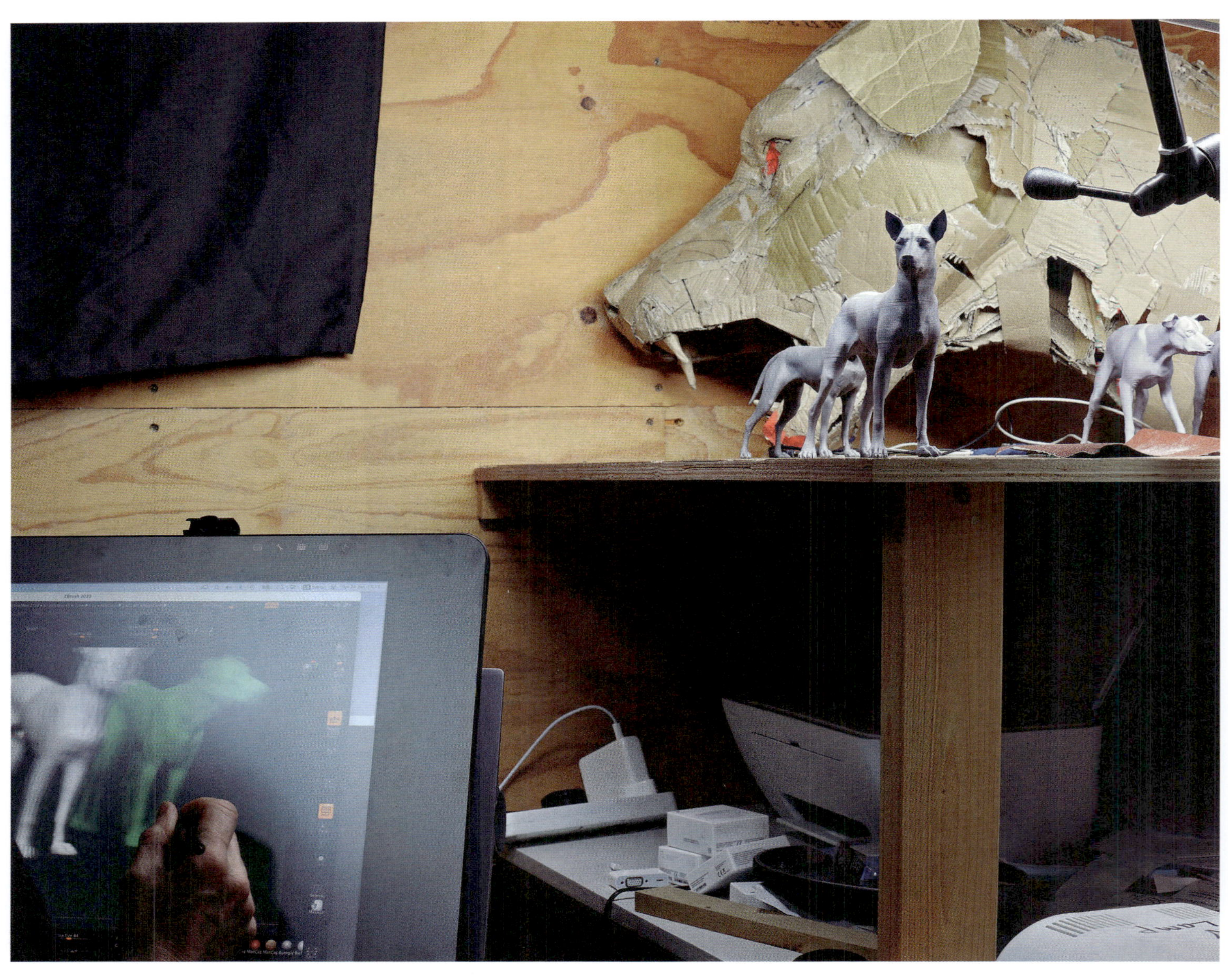

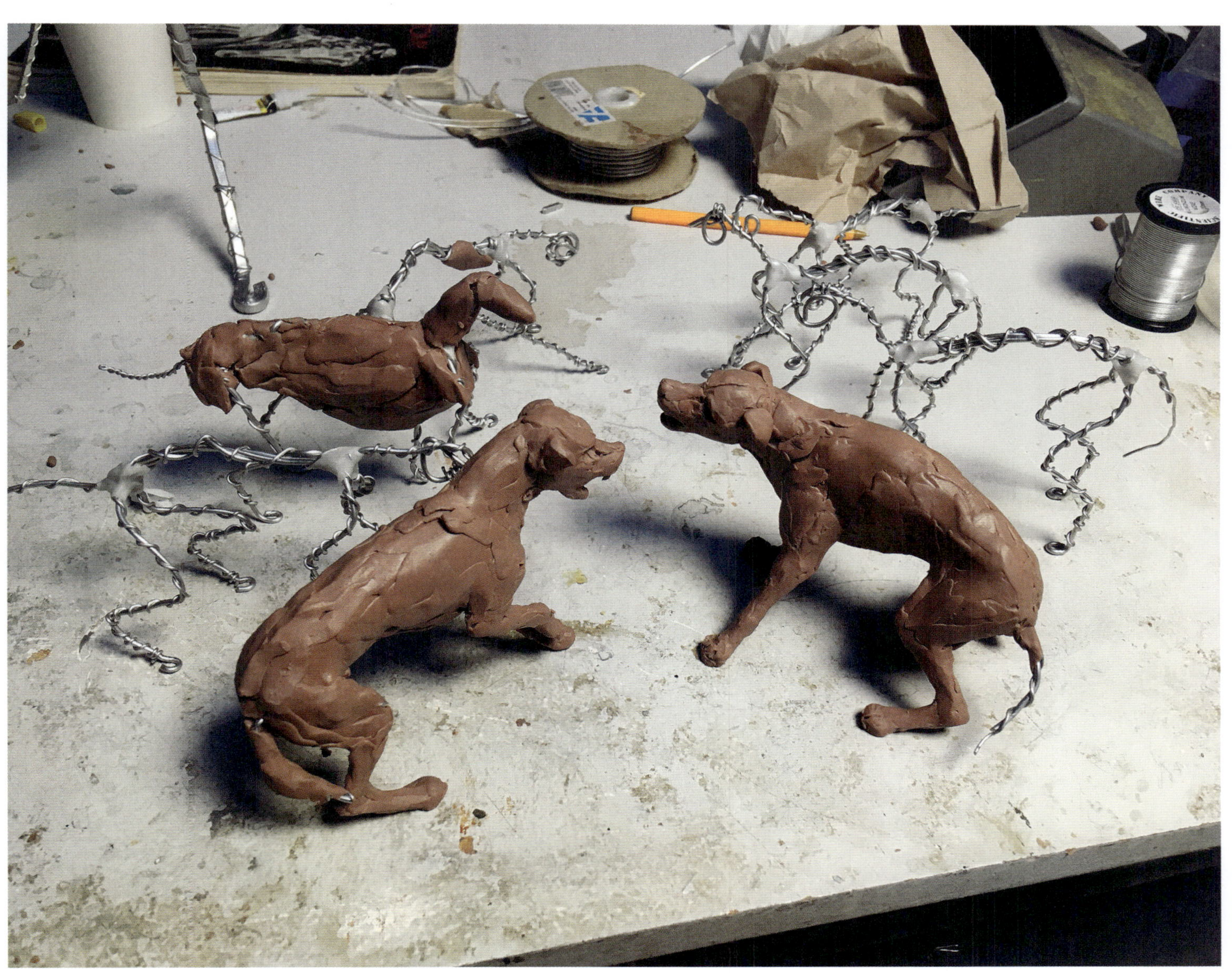

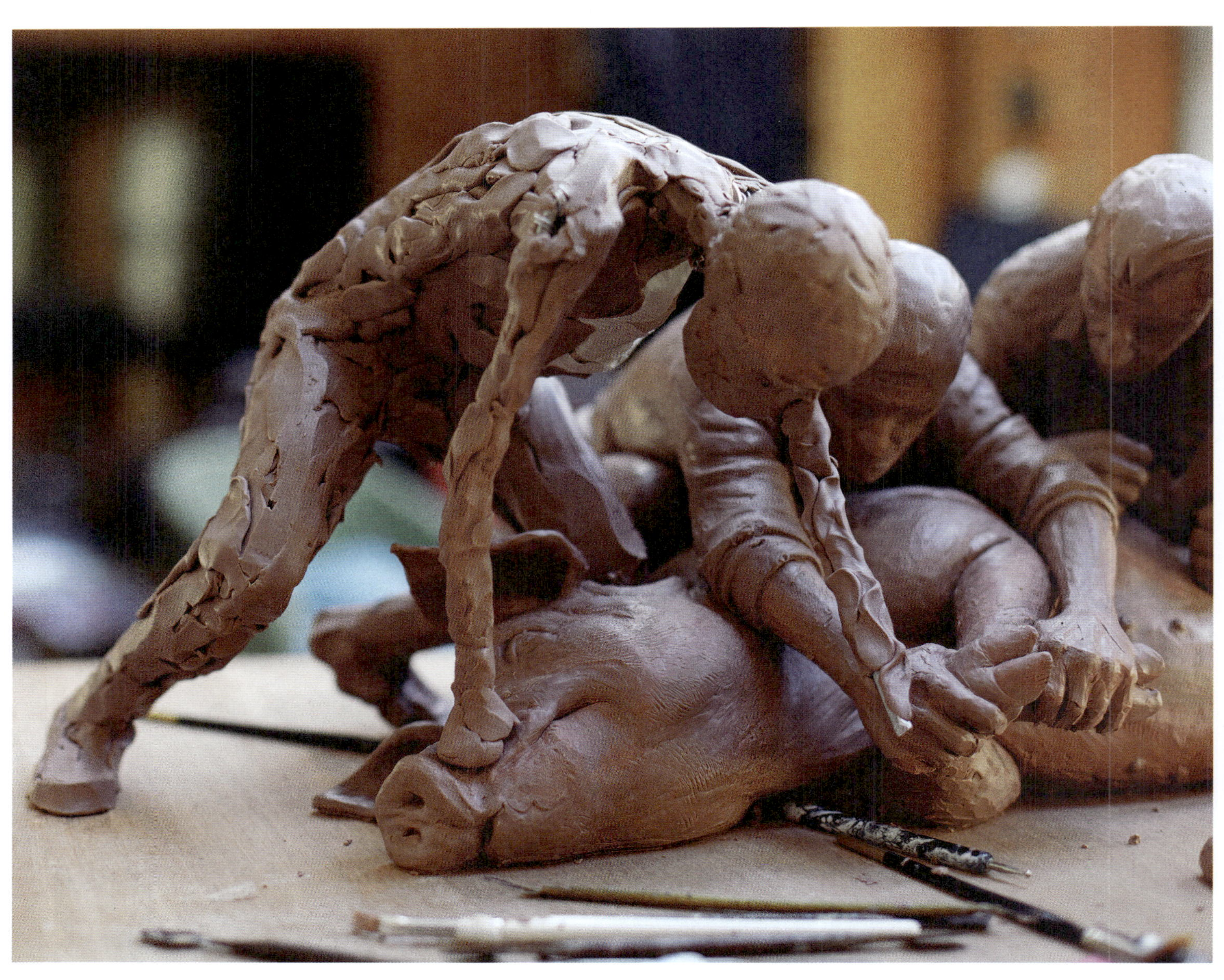

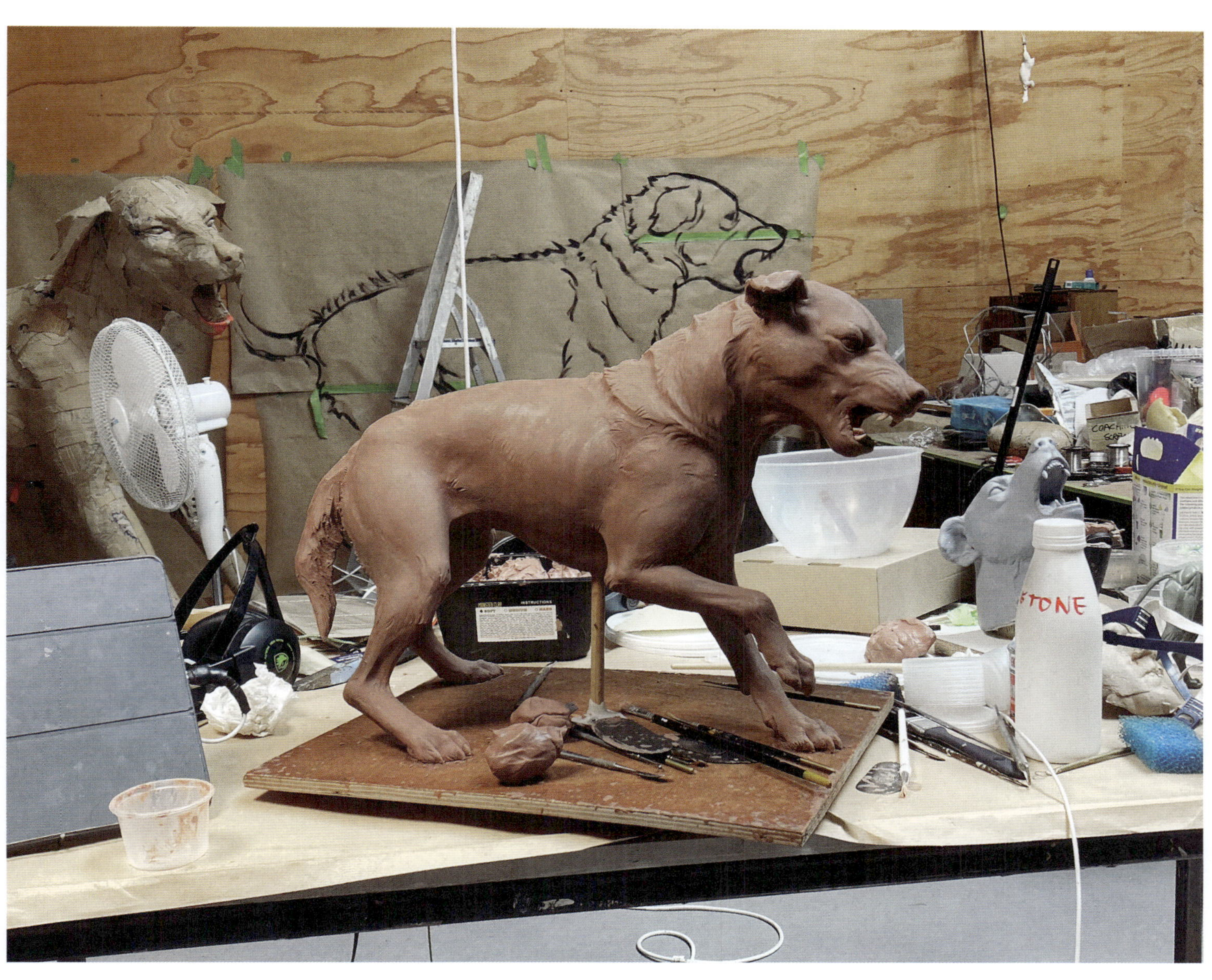

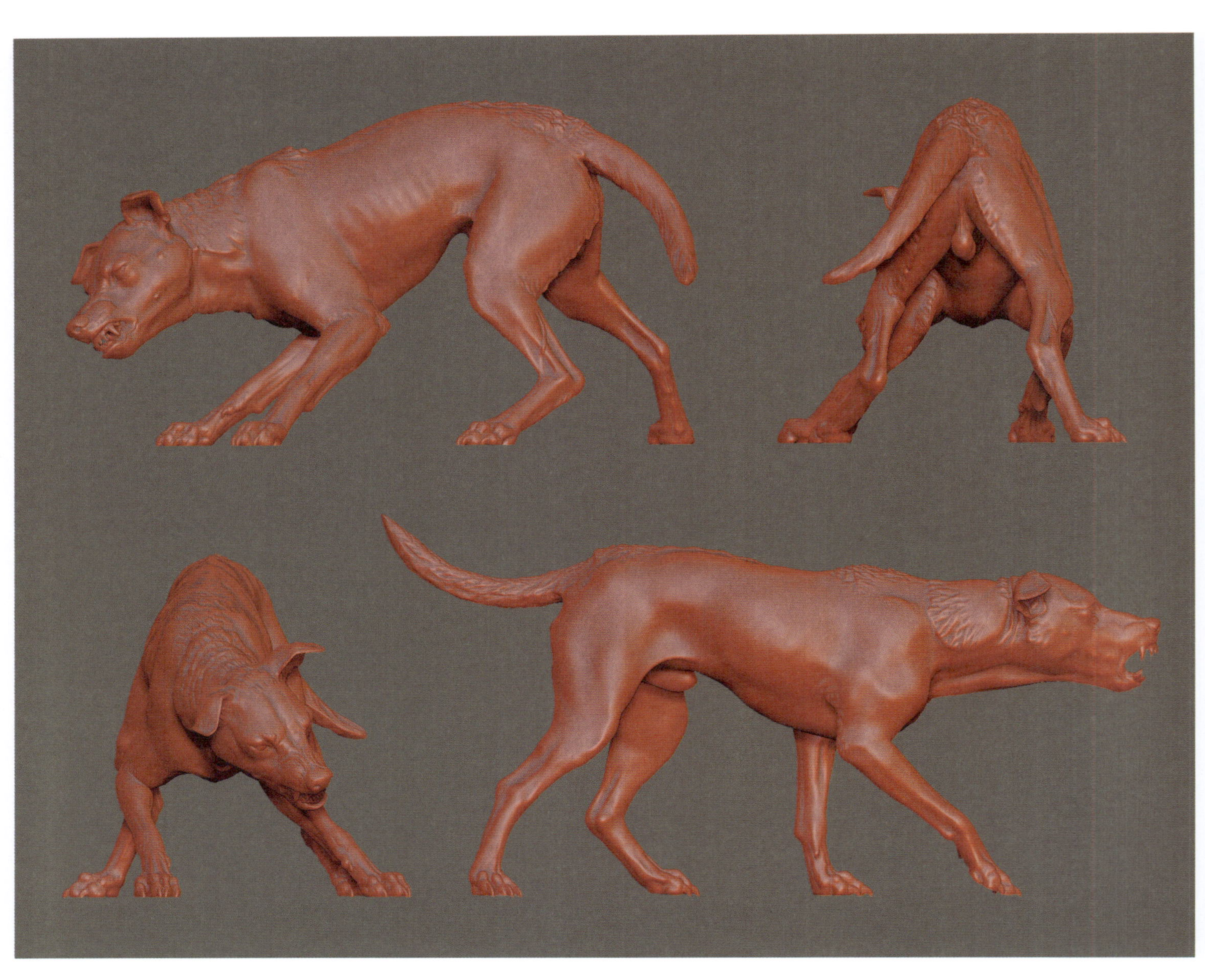

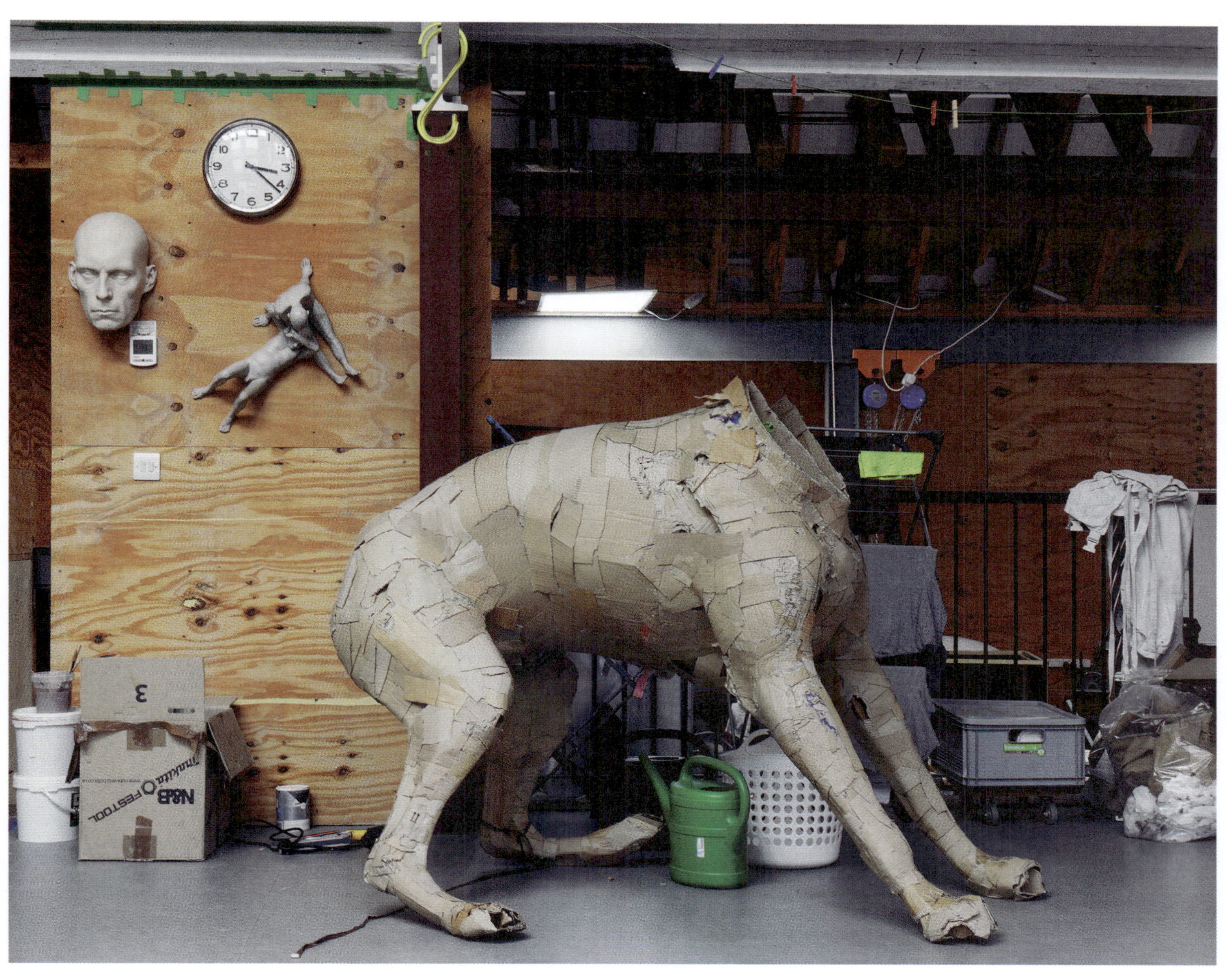

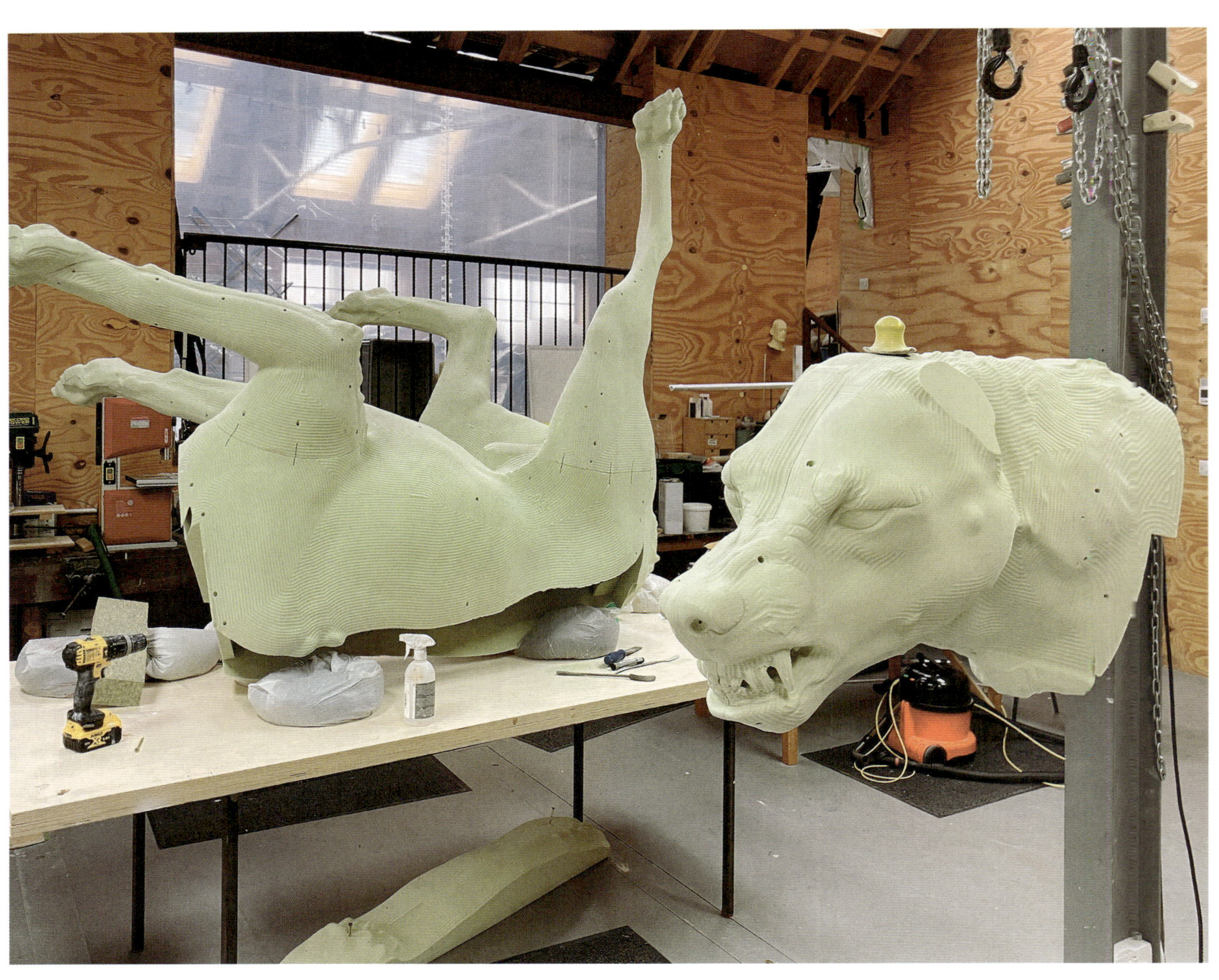

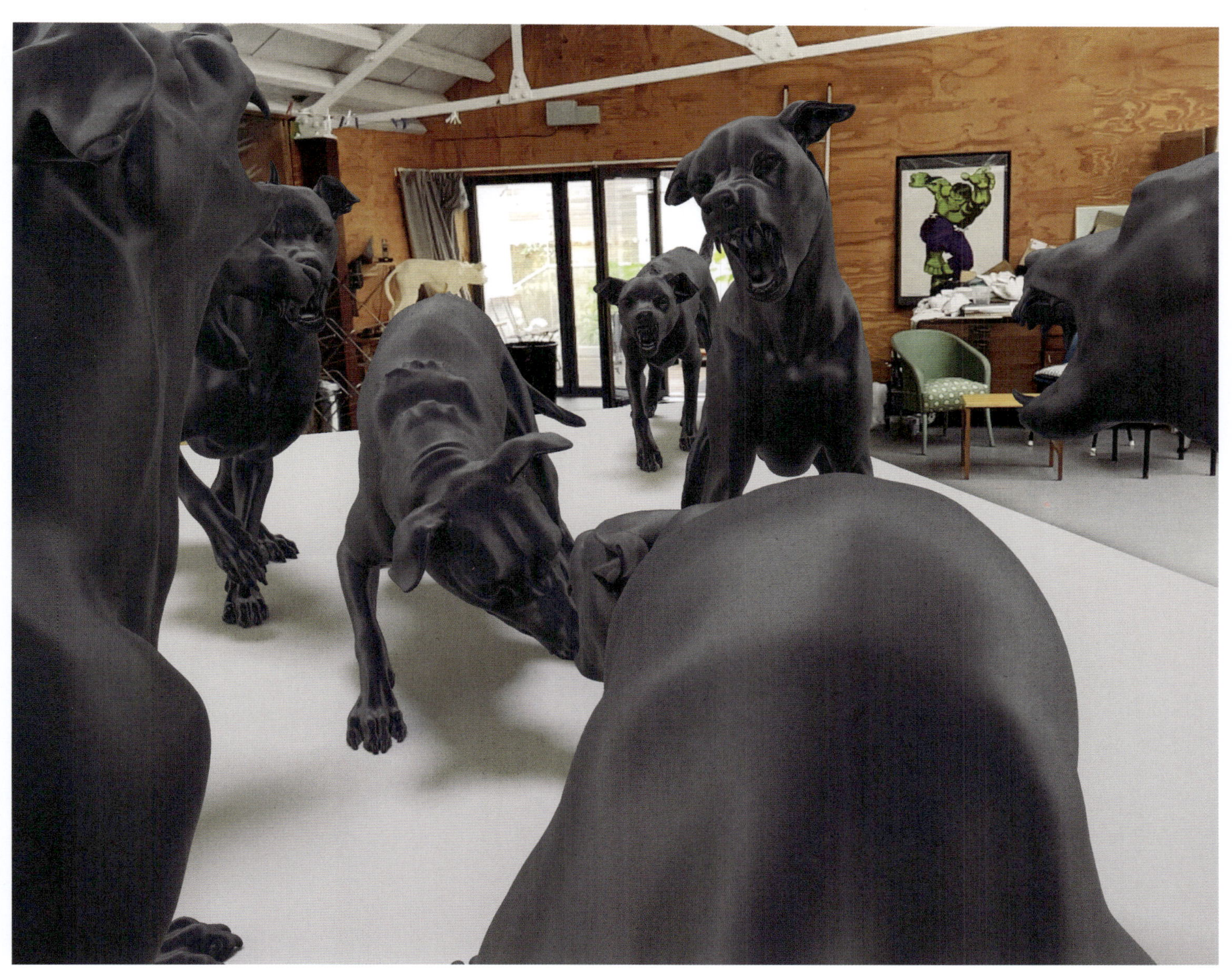

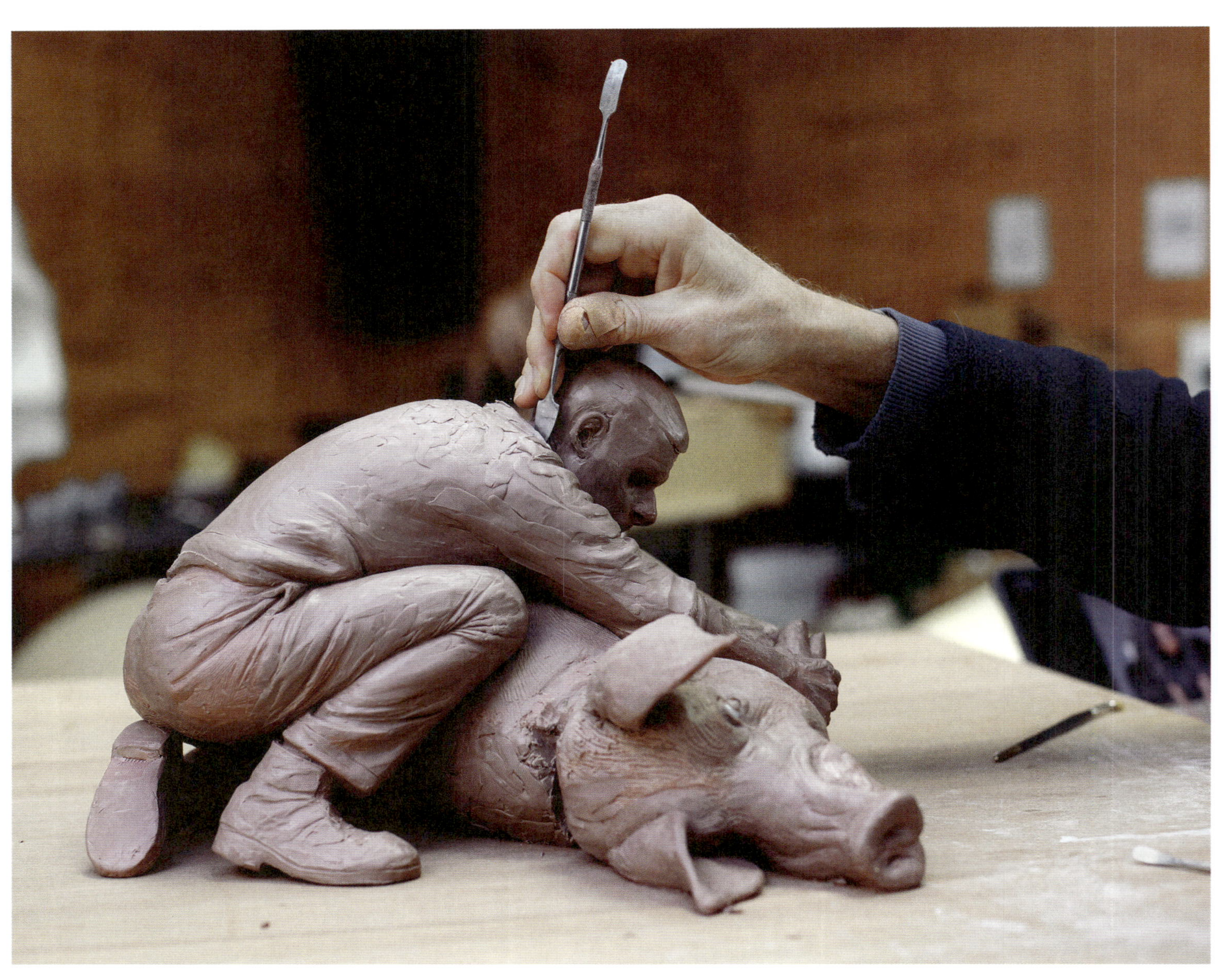

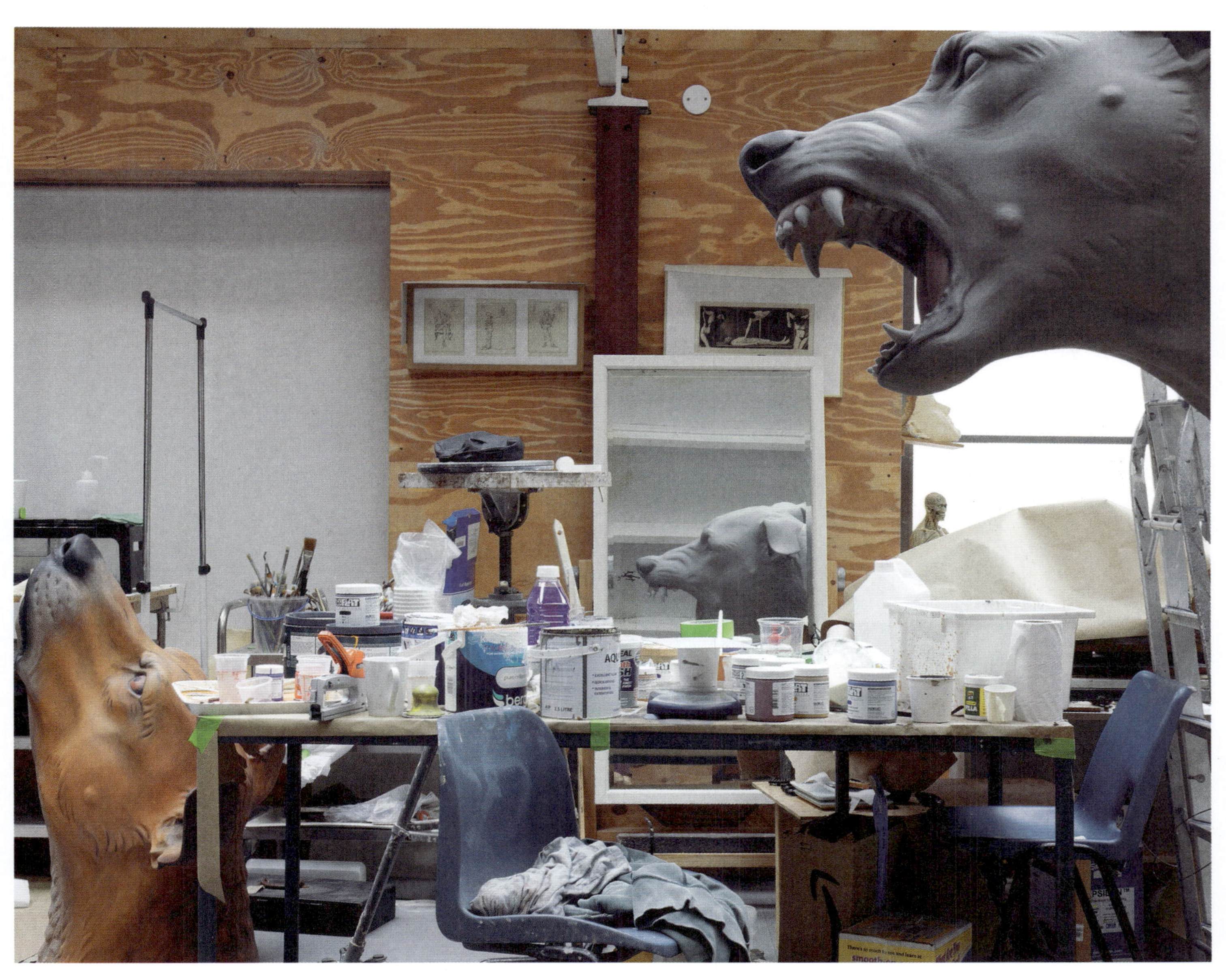

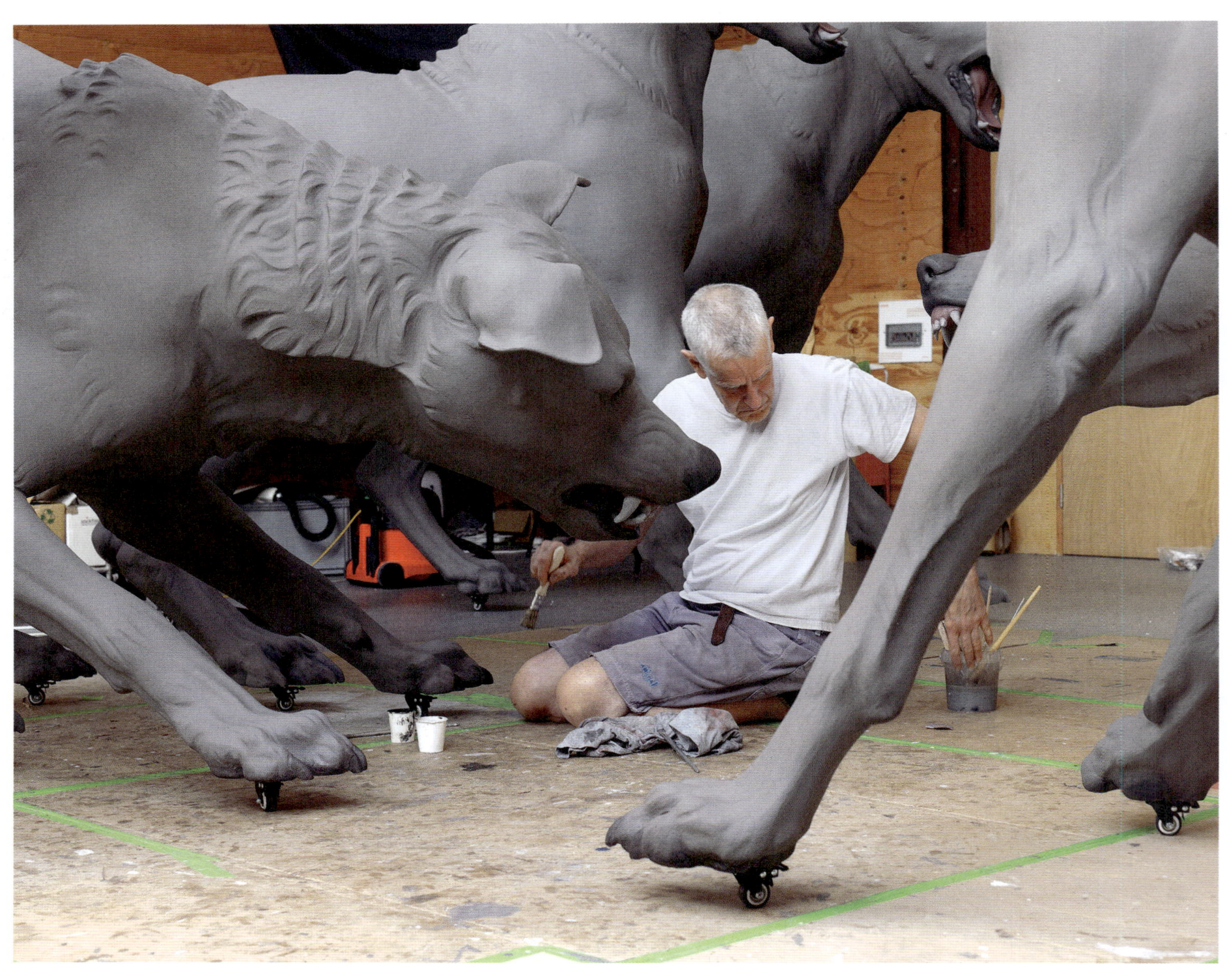

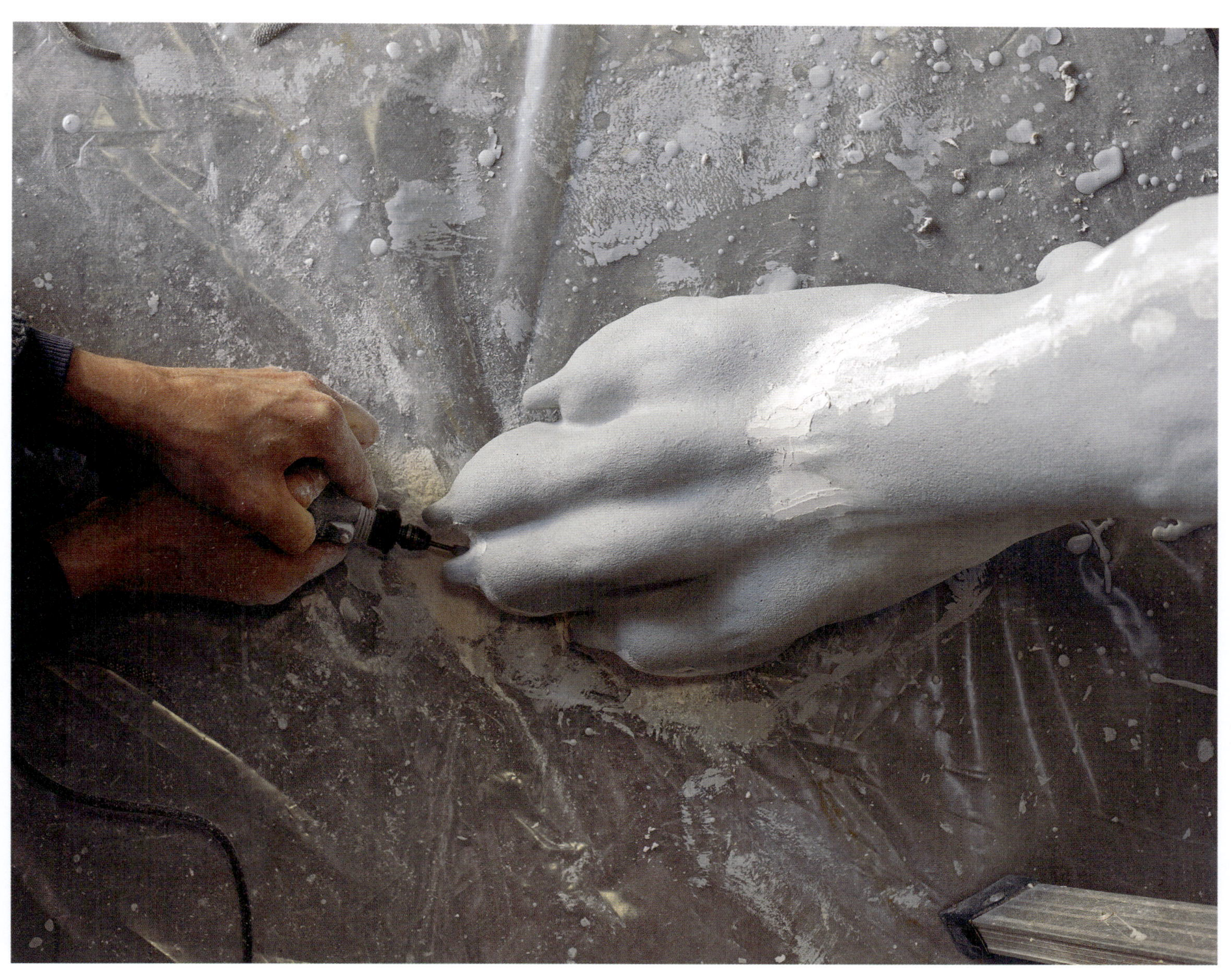

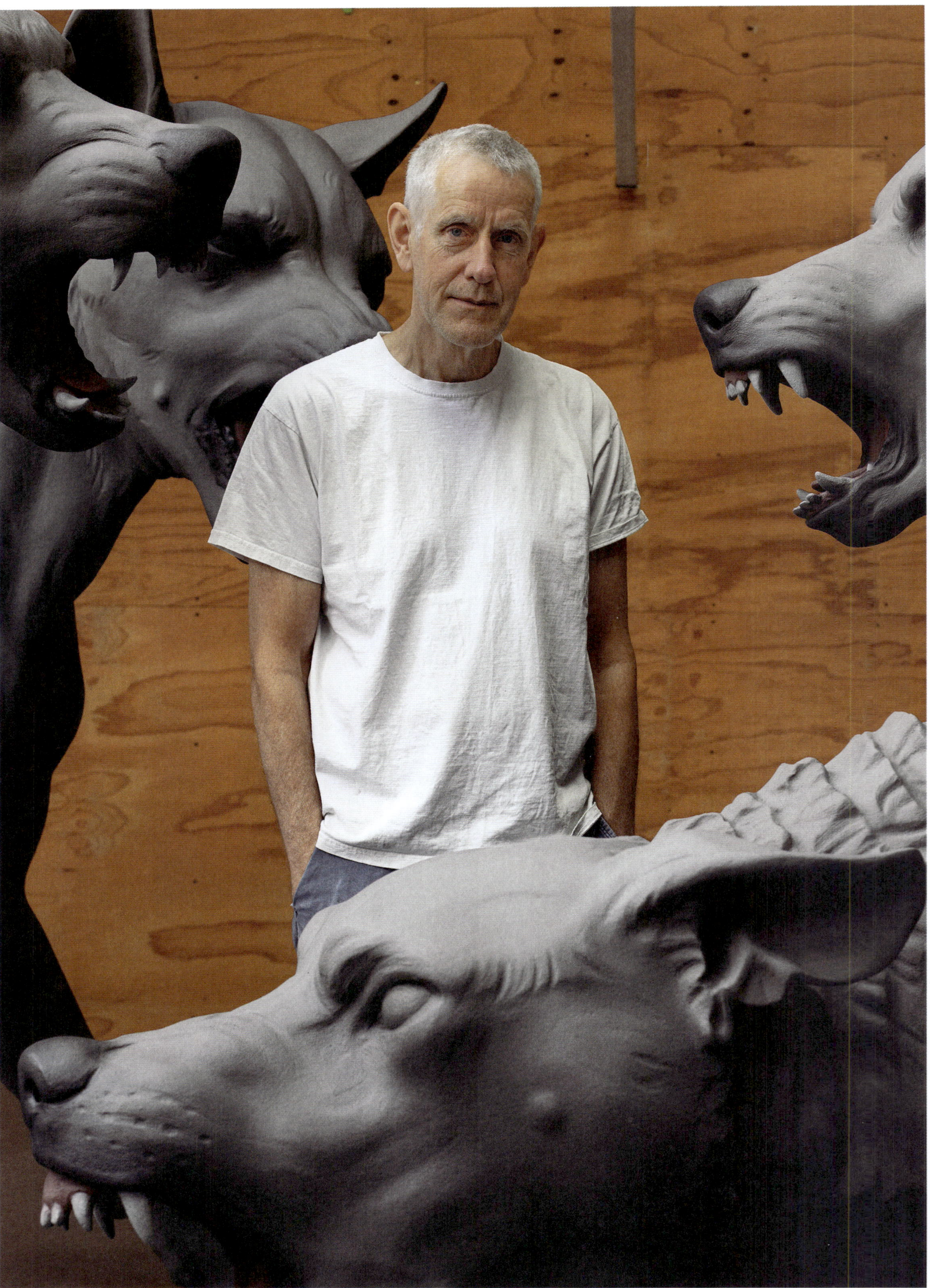

Ron Mueck was born in Melbourne in 1958 to German parents. As a child, he assisted in the family toy-making business.

Mueck began his career in the film and television industry; Australian audiences may recall his puppeteering on the children's program *Shirl's neighbourhood*. This was followed by work as a puppet-maker and puppeteer for American filmmaker Jim Henson, first in New York and then London, where Mueck worked on the cult 1986 film *Labyrinth*. Mueck stayed in London and shortly after began a successful business making models and puppets for advertising. In 1996, he collaborated with his mother-in-law, the celebrated painter Paula Rego, by sculpting a Pinocchio figure as a model for her paintings on that subject. Mueck's sculpture was exhibited alongside Rego's paintings in the exhibition *Spellbound: Art and Film* at the Hayward Gallery, which led to collector Charles Saatchi commissioning further works from him.

Mueck's career as a visual artist took off with *Dead Dad* 1996–97. This work, a tiny and haunting effigy of his deceased father, gained attention at the influential *Sensation: Young British Artists from the Saatchi Collection* exhibition at London's Royal Academy of Arts in 1997, which also travelled to Berlin and New York. The positive critical and popular response to Mueck's work established his reputation.

From 2000, Mueck spent two years as resident artist at London's National Gallery, working on pieces such as *Big Man* 2000, *Man in Blankets* 2000 and *Pregnant Woman* 2002. In the ensuing years, he became recognised as one of Australia's most internationally successful contemporary artists.

Mueck's sculptures are housed in some of the world's most important public museums and private collections. His work has been shown in exhibitions at prominent institutions around the world, most recently at the National Museum of Modern and Contemporary Art (MMCA), Seoul, Korea (2025), museum Voorlinden, Wassenaar, the Netherlands (2024) and Fondation Cartier pour l'art contemporain, Paris, France (2023). His solo exhibitions have broken visitor attendance records several times, including at Museu de Arte Moderna do Rio de Janeiro and Pinacoteca do Estado de Sao Paulo in Brazil (both 2014), and most recently at MMCA, Seoul (2025). Mueck's work has also been a crucial and much-admired inclusion in major global exhibitions on contemporary figurative sculpture, and he has often been among only a handful of twenty-first-century artists in more wide-reaching historical surveys.

Ron Mueck: Encounter reframes the artist's practice as one that, while evolving from the immaculate replication of surface detail to a focus on the essential form of dynamic groups, remains grounded in empathy, affect and our embodied experience. Including the launch of *Havoc* 2025 and the newly cast *This Little Piggy* 2023–25, *Encounter* is the equal-largest showing of Mueck's sculptures to date.

Dimensions are in centimetres,
height × width × depth.

Ron Mueck
Born 1958, Melbourne, Australia
Lives and works England

Ghost
1998/2014
artist's proof
mixed media
202 × 65 × 99 cm
YAGEO Foundation Collection,
Taipei

Crouching Boy in Mirror
1999–2002
edition 1/1
mixed media
43 × 46 × 28 cm figure;
46 × 56 cm mirror
The Broad Art Foundation,
Santa Monica

Man in Blankets
2000
edition 1/1
mixed media
38 × 46 × 71 cm
Collection museum Voorlinden,
Wassenaar, the Netherlands

Big Man
2000
edition 1/1
mixed media
204 × 121 × 205 cm
Hirshhorn Museum and
Sculpture Garden, Smithsonian
Institution, Washington, DC,
museum purchase with funds
provided by the Joseph H
Hirshhorn Bequest and in
honour of Robert Lehrman,
chairman of the Board of
Trustees, 1997–2004, for
his extraordinary leadership
and unstinting service to
the Hirshhorn Museum and
Sculpture Garden

Old Woman in Bed
2000/2002
artist's proof
mixed media
25 × 94 × 54 cm
Art Gallery of New South Wales,
Sydney, purchased 2003

Pregnant Woman
2002
edition 1/1
mixed media
252 × 78 × 72 cm
National Gallery of Australia,
Canberra, purchased with
the assistance of Tony and
Carol Berg 2003

Spooning Couple
2005
edition 1/1
mixed media
14 × 65 × 35 cm
Collection Glenn and
Amanda Fuhrman, New York,
courtesy the FLAG Art
Foundation

Woman with Sticks
2009–10
edition 1/1
mixed media
170 × 183 × 120 cm
Collection Fondation Cartier
pour l'art contemporain,
Paris, acquired 2013

Couple Under an Umbrella
2013
artist's proof
mixed media
275 × 455 × 330 cm
Giverny Capital Collection,
Montreal

Woman with Shopping
2013
edition 3/4
mixed media
113 × 46 × 30 cm
Collection Thaddaeus Ropac

Young Couple
2013
artist's proof
mixed media
89 × 43 × 23 cm
YAGEO Foundation Collection,
Taipei

Dark Place
2018
edition 1/1
mixed media
140 × 90 × 75 cm
ZAMU, Amsterdam

chicken/man
2019
edition 1/1
mixed media
80 × 140 × 86 cm
Collection of Christchurch
Art Gallery Te Puna o
Waiwhetū, purchased 2019
by Christchurch Art Gallery
Foundation with assistance
from Catherine and David Boyer,
Friends of Christchurch Art
Gallery Te Puna o Waiwhetū,
Charlotte and Marcel Gray,
Ben Gough Family Foundation,
Jenny and Andrew Smith,
Gabrielle Tasman and Ken
Lawn, Christchurch Art Gallery
Foundation's London Club
along with 514 other generous
individuals and companies

This Little Piggy
2023–25
edition 1/1
mixed media
70 × 90 × 30 cm
Courtesy the artist

Havoc
2025
edition 1/1
mixed media
dimensions variable
Courtesy the artist
Ron Mueck thanks all those
involved in the making of *Havoc*

Acknowledgements

Curating an exhibition with artist Ron Mueck has been an honour and a pleasure. I thank Ron for revealing his potent new work, *Havoc*, for the first time in Sydney, alongside major pieces from throughout his career. I congratulate him for courageously testing himself through vital new directions in his practice. Ron's rigour and craftsmanship are matched by an empathic intelligence and social conscience that tenderly holds focus on our shared humanity.

I warmly acknowledge Ron's exhibitions director, Charlie Clarke, whose ever helpful and insightful contribution has been immeasurable. Charlie has been an exceptional collaborator on every aspect of the exhibition, driven by a determined commitment to best represent Ron and ensure the perfect presentation of each one of his extraordinary works. He has been, in addition, a warm and thoughtful colleague who truly stands as a co-creator of our exhibition.

I acknowledge Polly Robinson Gaer, executive director of Thaddaeus Ropac, London, who has enthusiastically and supportively guided the planning of the exhibition from its inception, including crucial liaison with lenders. I also thank James Elliott, director of collections at Anthony d'Offay Ltd, London, and Anthony d'Offay himself, for their support of Ron's practice.

For his contribution to this catalogue and exhibition, my profound thanks go to photographer and filmmaker Gautier Deblonde. After twenty years of working beautifully together, Gautier and Ron once again met in the studio to document a new work in development.

The production of this catalogue and the exhibition *Ron Mueck: Encounter* has involved the talents of dedicated staff from across the Art Gallery of New South Wales. Chief among them is director Maud Page, whose inspirational vision to bring Ron Mueck back to Australia, dating back to 2017, kicked off a journey for us both. I wish to extend my thanks to her executive team, including Wayne Tunnicliffe, acting director of collections, as well as Justin Paton, head curator of international art.

In particular from the exhibition project team, I would like to thank exhibition manager Fatima Hijazi for her quietly efficient leadership; exhibition registrar Kate Beckingham for her apparently effortless wrangling of international loans, and exhibition designers Jemima Woo and Isaac Harrisson for a design that presents Ron's sculptures in his desired manner: simply, crisply and spaciously, so they may speak all the more clearly. My thanks too to photographer Felicity Jenkins, lighting technician Jaye Ottens and lead installer John Freckleton, and my appreciation to the head of exhibitions, Charlotte Cox, for her unwavering practical and personal support.

I thank editorial manager Faith Chisholm for her guidance and editor Lisa Girault for her thoughtful editing of this publication and all exhibition texts, graphic designer Elliott Bryce Foulkes for the creation of this beautiful volume and his fine work on the exhibition graphics, and my rights and image licensing colleagues, Megan Young and Marina Colagrossi. Beyond them, my thanks go to each of my colleagues at the Art Gallery who has helped to make this exhibition both possible and outstanding.

I reserve my special thanks for the lenders, who have so generously assisted us in realising this exhibition. Releasing a beloved, and in all senses fragile, work for a period of months is hard, be it an institution – whose audiences clamour to see 'their Ron Mueck' – or a private collection – whose owners may miss keenly a Mueck figure's presence as part of their family home or foundation. I wish to thank the owners and collection staff of: The Broad Art Foundation, Santa Monica; Christchurch Art Gallery Te Puna o Waiwhetū; Collection Fondation Cartier pour l'art contemporain, Paris; Collection Glenn and Amanda Fuhrman, New York; Giverny Capital Collection, Montreal; Hirshhorn Museum and Sculpture Garden, Smithsonian Institution, Washington, DC; National Gallery of Australia, Canberra; Thaddaeus Ropac; Collection museum Voorlinden, Wassenaar, the Netherlands; YAGEO Foundation Collection, Taipei; and ZAMU, Amsterdam. For the loan of the exhilarating new works *This Little Piggy* and *Havoc*, may I thank the artist, courtesy of Thaddaeus Ropac, London – Paris – Salzburg – Seoul – Milan.

I am grateful to Destination NSW, supporter of the Sydney International Art Series, which brings ambitious exhibitions to local audiences. Through *Encounter* thousands more can fall under the spell of Ron Mueck's humane and enchanting practice.

Jackie Dunn
Senior curator, exhibitions
Art Gallery of New South Wales

Internationally celebrated artist Ron Mueck creates captivating figures, scaled from the minute to the monumental, embodying themes such as birth and death, and alienation and togetherness, which invite us to explore our relationship with the world.

Ron Mueck: Encounter is the largest exhibition of Mueck's work ever to be presented in Australia, including a dramatic new immersive work that has been created specifically for this occasion.

Encounter is part of the annual Sydney International Art Series – a collaboration between the NSW Government's tourism and major events agency, Destination NSW; the Museum of Contemporary Art Australia; and the Art Gallery of New South Wales – which brings the world's most exceptional artists and their works exclusively to Sydney, reinforcing our city's reputation as a global hub for cultural experiences.

I commend the Art Gallery of New South Wales for the development of *Encounter* and thank the artist and lenders whose collaboration and support has made this exhibition possible.

The Hon Steve Kamper MP
Minister for Lands and Property
Minister for Multiculturalism
Minister for Sport
Minister for Jobs and Tourism

SYDNEY INTERNATIONAL ART SERIES

NSW GOVERNMENT

Strategic sponsor

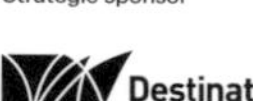

Major partner

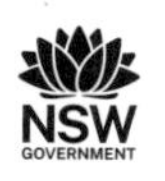

Media partners

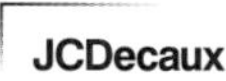

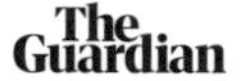

Published by
Art Gallery of New South Wales
on Gadigal Country
Art Gallery Road, The Domain
Sydney NSW 2000, Australia
artgallery.nsw.gov.au

in association with the exhibition
Ron Mueck: Encounter
Art Gallery of New South Wales, Sydney
6 December 2025 – 12 April 2026

A catalogue record for this book is available
from the National Library of Australia
ISBN 978 1 74174 182 7

Publishing manager: Faith Chisholm
Managing editor: Lisa Girault
Text editing: Lisa Girault
Rights and permissions:
Marina Colagrossi and Megan Young
Proofreading: Melissa Ratliff
Production: Cara Hickman
Prepress: Spitting Image
Printed in China by
Australian Book Connection

The Art Gallery of New South Wales
is a statutory body of the NSW State
Government.

Front cover: *Crouching Boy in Mirror*
1999–2002 (detail)
Back cover: *Woman with Sticks*
2009–10 (detail)

Distribution:
Thames & Hudson Australia
Thames & Hudson UK
University of Washington Press USA